Mohamed A. G. Bakhit

Identity and Lifestyle Construction in Multi-ethnic Shantytowns

Beiträge zur Afrikaforschung

ISSN 0938–7285

Herausgegeben vom Institut für Afrikastudien

in Verbindung mit der
Bayreuth International Graduate School of African Studies, BIGSAS
der Universität Bayreuth

Band

64

LIT

Mohamed A. G. Bakhit

Identity and Lifestyle Construction in Multi-ethnic Shantytowns

A Case Study of Al-Baraka Community in Khartoum, Sudan

LIT

Printed with the support of the German Research Foundation
(Deutsche Forschungsgemeinschaft), DFG

Bibliographic information published by the Deutsche Nationalbibliothek
The Deutsche Nationalbibliothek lists this publication in the Deutsche Nationalbibliografie; detailed bibliographic data are available in the Internet at http://dnb.d-nb.de.

ISBN 978-3-643-90677-9
Zugl.: Bayreuth, Univ., BIGSAS, 2014

A catalogue record for this book is available from the British Library

Fresnostr. 2
D-48159 Münster
Tel. +49 (0) 2 51-62 03 20
Fax +49 (0) 2 51-23 19 72
E-Mail: lit@lit-verlag.de
http://www.lit-verlag.de

LIT VERLAG GmbH & Co. KG Wien,
Zweigniederlassung Zürich 2015
Klosbachstr. 107
CH-8032 Zürich
Tel. +41 (0) 44-251 75 05
Fax +41 (0) 44-251 75 06
E-Mail: zuerich@lit-verlag.ch
http://www.lit-verlag.ch

Distribution:
In the UK: Global Book Marketing, e-mail: mo@centralbooks.com
In North America: International Specialized Book Services, e-mail: orders@isbs.com
In Germany: LIT Verlag Fresnostr. 2, D-48159 Münster
Tel. +49 (0) 2 51-620 32 22, Fax +49 (0) 2 51-922 60 99, E-mail: vertrieb@lit-verlag.de

In Austria: Medienlogistik Pichler-ÖBZ, e-mail: mlo@medien-logistik.at
e-books are available at www.litwebshop.de

Table of Contents

Acknowledgments

This study would not have been possible without support and guidance from several people and institutions. My immense gratitude goes to my supervisor Prof. Kurt Beck for his excellent supervision through his advice, patience and commitment in supervising this thesis, reading through the drafts and making the necessary corrections. His many comments, insightful suggestions and critical reviews made the study much easier and better.

Foremost I acknowledge the immeasurable guidance, advice and constant academic support from the mentoring of Prof. George Klute. Thanks also to the members of the PhD committee for their constructive comments on the manuscript of the thesis.

I am most grateful to the people from Al-Baraka community who shaped the study to what it is now. They were more than informants. In fact they were partners, teachers and mentors. They welcomed me with open arms and hearts to their houses, to their social events, and to their public meetings. The fieldwork experience in Al-Baraka area re-shaped me personally, as much as it shaped this thesis.

This thesis would not have been successful without the support of the German Academic Exchange Service (DAAD) for a three and half year fund to pursue my studies at the University of Bayreuth, Germany. In addition, I wish to particularly thank the Bayreuth International Graduate School of African Studies (BIGSAS) for the scholarship award to pursue my doctorate studies, besides a one year preparatory course and the opportunity to acquire valuable skills through seminars, workshops, and conferences.

I wish to thank my employer, the University of Khartoum, Sudan, specifically the Department of Anthropology for allowing me study leave to pursue my doctorate. Special thanks also go to my colleagues in the department for their immense academic and social support.

I offer a special thanks to Nicki Kindersley for her valuable efforts in language editing and proofreading. Without her help throughout the last stages of the thesis it would be far more difficult to reach this level of language quality.

Most importantly, I am grateful to my family for their support and constant encouragement: my wonderful father Abdelbagi, my lovely mother Shadia, my brothers and sisters and their families for their love, immense words of support. I wish also to especially thank my friends and colleagues in Bayreuth and Sudan for their support and encouragement throughout my studies.

Mohamed A. G. Bakhit, Bayreuth, 20/4/2015

List of Figures

Glossary

IDPs	Internally Displaced Persons
NGOs	Non-Governmental Organizations
CBOs	Community-Based Organizations
al-muhatta	A hangout place for young people
zibâla	A mixture of fermented mud, dry grass and dung
rakûba	Traditional verandah made of straw and empty sacks
marîsa	Locally produced sorghum beer
aragi	Locally distilled lcohol
SDG	Sudanese Pound
SPLM/A	Sudanese People Liberation Movement/Army
Sultan	An ethnic group leader
Sheikh	Religious or ethnic leader
Khalwa	A traditional Islamic school teaching the Qur'an for children
Eid Ramadan	Three days of celebration after fasting for the holy month of Ramadan
Imam	A religious leader who leads ceremonies in the mosque
Negarz	Youth gangs
agânî al-banât	Women's songs
agânî tarab	Enjoyable songs
NCP	National Congress Party
Hakuma	The government, or the people who represent the government
agânî habit	Low quality singing

Abstract

This thesis examines the construction of identity and different lifestyles of the Al-Baraka shantytown area, located in the north-eastern periphery of Khartoum city in Sudan, populated mainly by migrants and Internally Displaced Persons (IDPs) from South Sudan, Darfur and the Nuba Mountains. The study focuses on the processes of social identity construction and practiced lifestyles of shantytown settlers, on the bases of generational variations, rural-urban disparities, and ethno-cultural differences between Khartoum city and local people's home areas in south and western Sudan.

Academic literature has usually depicted Sudan as a country suffering from a 'crisis of identity', with this troubled identity usually explained in the form of three binary oppositions: on an ethnic basis, as African vs. Arab, or a religious basis, as Islam vs. Christianity and traditional beliefs, or on a linguistic basis, as Arabic language vs. traditional languages.

This research is an ethnographic study; accordingly, I used participant observation as the main method to collect empirical data. I rented two houses in different Quarters of Al Baraka (No. 2, and No. 4), each for six months (April-September 2010, and October 2011-March 2012 respectively), and tried to follow the daily life, activities and events for different groups and individuals living in those areas. For this, I used unstructured interviews, group discussions, audio recordings, reports, photography, genealogies, social network diagrams, and academic literature as the basis for my work. Analysis of the data was based on extensive listening and transcribing of the interviews and group discussions, besides depending on field notes. I used those resources to develop the main concepts and categories of the study. In later analytical stages, I use the concepts of lifestyle and the localization process as basic tools of analysis to develop a theoretical model that can be applied to other comparable communities in the global South. This theoretical model is supported by extensive verification methods from firsthand data collected in the field, and literature from anthropological studies and various other disciplines.

In my first days in the field, I asked people about the way they defined themselves and others; all my informants agreed that they usually use ethnic identification as the primary basis of classification, as everybody knows his or her ethnic group, and many people are called after their tribal names. However, with more experience in the field, I came to realize that many people may identify themselves as from one ethnic group but actually perform different daily practices, hold different values and perceptions, and in fact share very little in common. For this reason, I started to use 'lifestyle' as the main concept to analyze and categorize the different social groups that co-exist in Al-Baraka area. This also enabled me to differentiate between a verbal identity, where people use ethnicity as a basis of identification, and actual identity, or the total performances and social practices of individuals and groups, as their lifestyles.

According to this categorization, in Al-Baraka, I identified three basic lifestyle groups in the shantytown: the first generation, educated people, and the second generation. These lifestyle groups formed as direct results of the specific variables that created the shantytown settle-

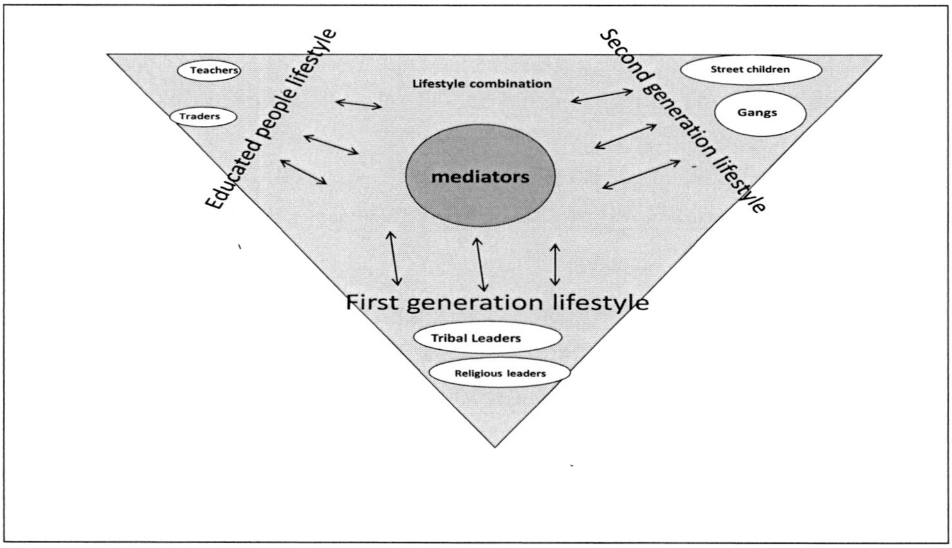

ment. These social groups were based upon certain ways of life pursued by their members.

The best way to illustrate the relationships between these three ways of life is through a triangular diagram (see Figure below). Each lifestyle could stand as a distinctive social entity, in the sense that it has a specific structure and a unique lifestyle. More importantly, each lifestyle group has its own legitimacy and recognition by other lifestyle members, regardless of whether that recognition takes the form of appreciation or condemnation.

In each corner of the triangle lies one of the three distinct lifestyles, with people scattered inside the triangle, some of whom are more attached to one 'corner' (e.g. gangs, teachers, tribal leaders). This means that these 'corner' groups close off their social relations and daily practices within their own small group, and they are less likely to interact with people practicing other lifestyles.

The majority of the population has positioned themselves between more than one extreme corner, and so are invested in some elements of more than one way of life. There are also others who are in the middle of the triangle, who embracing elements of all three lifestyles; these people are generally considered as more popular people (i.e. as mediators).

For the majority of the population, opting for only one lifestyle is not an ideal option. People tend to combine two or three lifestyles at the same time, and this is exactly what makes this population distinct from their urban neighbors, as well as their home area ancestors and relatives. This is what gives shantytowns a unique overall identity, which represents what people actually perceive as 'good' or 'ideal' daily life activities and practices in the Al-Baraka environment.

The research findings suggest that it is possible to use the concept of localization—instead of assimilation—to interpret the whole process of the adoption and internalization of different kinds of institutions and sets of practices by Al-Baraka people from different sources. This is visible within the realm of lifestyles, whereby each group tried to adopt as much as possible of local ideas and practices to establish its legitimacy, and attract more people to join the group in their specific lifestyle.

The concept of localization process appears vital to understanding how Al-Baraka people adopt different kinds of behaviors, institutions and activities from various origins and re-invent them locally to be their own, thus removing any sense of alienation. Through gradual processes of localization and domestication, this moves these social practices from being exclusively introduced and used by a minority in the extreme corners of the social triangle to towards the center, where increasingly more people accept the practice or become part of it. In order for this to happen, many changes and modifications need to be incorporated to the original idea. Accordingly, the research examines three examples drawn from the three social lifestyles that dominate in the shantytowns (Nuba wrestling, rickshaw driving, and private schooling).

It is possible to extend this further, and use the localization process to interpret the wider situation: that is, the congregation of lifestyles adopted by people, otherwise termed their whole social identity. When we try to make generalizations about the whole population of the shantytowns, in fact, we are talking about localization on a community scale, or more precisely about the shantytowns vis-à-vis other communities.

When Al-Baraka people interact with themselves and the environment around them, they encounter other identities (i.e. different lifestyles) from their original areas, from urban surroundings, or even from the outside world through technology and media. None of those proposed identities could satisfy their exact social needs, but are still the sources of the specific identity under construction and localization.

People used their agency to move freely between those different options, or more precisely different lifestyles, and make their choices according to their needs, by modifying and localizing different sets of identities through social practices. This process crafts a new invented identity (i.e. through practiced lifestyles) out of all the different options available and already adopted by various sizes of lifestyle groups.

The construction of a shantytown social identity, according to this analysis, is a result of continuous interactions and exchanges between the local community and outside world(s). Through different local groups and specific lifestyles, engaged in endless localization processes, the ultimate result is a sort of social identity unique to all world(s) that contributed to the existence of the shantytown. The localization of the identity of the shantytown community is a nucleus example of what is happening in all different communities across the Sudan, or across the global South in general.

This thesis therefore concludes that the social identity of Sudan today is certainly not confined to the simplistic binary opposition (e.g. Arab vs. African), but is constituted of social identities comprised of more complex sets of practiced lifestyles. Those practiced lifestyles informed and communicated with all the world(s) that Sudan's society is or has been related to, in the past or the present.

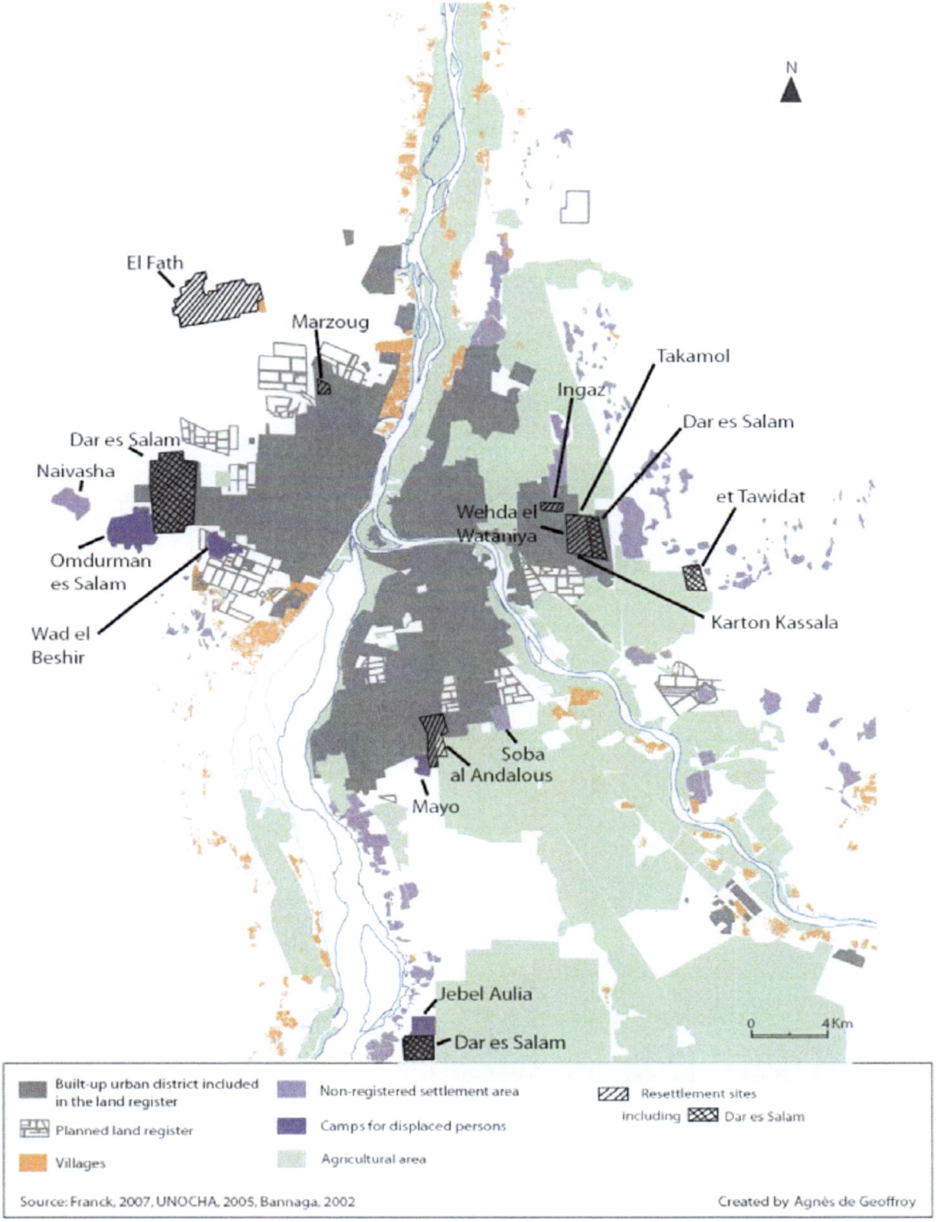

Figure 1: Map of Shantytowns in Khartoum

Chapter 1: Introduction

1.1 Introduction

Nowadays, there is a strong academic focus on identity politics as the main factor causing armed conflicts and man-made disasters around the world. In the Sudan, recent studies suggest that there is an identity struggle at the national level between an Arabic/Islamic identity versus an African/non-Islamic identity (Deng 2005; De Waal 2005; Assal 2009; Idris 2005; O'Fahey 1996; Sharkey 2007). Conflicts and political instability have plagued the Sudan since its independence, and recently led to the split into two countries—Sudan and South Sudan—with these conflicts apparently based upon this identity divide; all other parts of the country still suffer from symptoms of this problem. This encourages academic exploration into Sudanese culture and communities to gain a better understanding of the 'identity crisis' of the Sudan, including the nature of 'the multiple marginality of the Sudan' (Mazrui 1971: 240).

More broadly, the question of 'identity' has attained a remarkable centrality within human and social sciences. In the field of sociology, for example, the dominance of 'class' as the fundamental basis of the social structure has been challenged by the presence of various new social theories, including feminism, post-colonialism and environmentalist approaches. In anthropology, there is an increasing focus on ethnic identity and identity politics, not only in third world countries, but also in Eastern Europe and North America. This is because the concept of identity appears more relevant to explain armed conflicts, political instability and cultural divisions around the world, despite many other concepts having been used to analyze and interpret these devastating situations (e.g. economic weakness, climatic changes).

1.2. Shantytowns in Khartoum

Despite its richness in resources, Sudan, like many other countries in sub-Saharan Africa, has witnessed many years of political instability and civil wars since its independence in 1956. The country has also suffered from many other prolonged problems, such as ethnic conflicts, high rates of poverty, vast population displacement, the unequal distribution of social services, high levels of immigration, many forms of environmental disasters and a poor quality of government services (education, healthcare, as well as low achievements in governmentality and rule of law).

Indeed, about 13.5 percent[1] of the total population of Sudan currently lives in the capital Khartoum (see Figure No. 2). Migrants to the capital city come from all parts of Sudan, due to its concentration of services and economic growth. The first waves of migrants arrived in the capital during the period of 1960-1980. These were economic migrants, the majority of whom originated from the Northern parts of the country, searching for employment in the newly established commercial and industrial sectors in the capital. The majority were educated, with only 23 percent of all migrants to Khartoum aged 20-24 years in 1971 without any education (Galal-aldin 1980). Most chose to live at the periphery of the city or in small villages near the city's boundaries, until these were gradually swallowed up by the urban area. The statistics show that a small number also came from areas in Western and Southern Sudan (between 5 and 8 percent) to work as unskilled workers, living near the industrial zones in illegal squatter settlements. Later on, the government, under pressure from local residents, forcibly removed them and planned a new legal fourth-class settlement on the outskirts of the city, which forms the nuclei of the present Wehda el Wataniya shantytowns.

The second wave of migrants arrived during 1980-2000, prompted by the civil war in the South and ethnic conflicts in Darfur, as well as drought and desertification in Western Sudan. About two million people were displaced from their original areas and relocated into the capital city. They lived in different areas, some on any vacant land within Khartoum; others preferred to settle at the periphery of the city, near old legal shantytowns, but the majority inhabited squatter settlements. One study estimates the number of illegal squatter settlements in Khartoum in 1991 as more than 50 settlements, occupied by about 1.5 million Internally Displaced Persons (IDPs) (Banaga 2001). While a recent study estimates that IDPs in Khartoum constitute between 18 and 23 percent of the total population (about 7 million), another report by UN Habitat classifies about 60 percent of the city's population as urban poor (see Figure No.1), from diverse settlement backgrounds (10% IDP camps, 10% squatter areas, 50% upgraded areas) (Pantuliano et al., 2011: 4-5).

The early history of shantytowns dates back to the 1960s: "By 1965 the growth of these settlements was posing a threat to the government. These already had 30,000 inhabitants, 20,000 of them in the Khartoum North area… In 1971 both areas were relocated. That of Khartoum was

[1] Statistical Year Book for the Year 2009, Central Bureau of Statistics, Republic of Sudan.

moved south of the Green Belt. The other one of Khartoum North was relocated in only 5 weeks at Haj Yousif, where 3,000 plots were prepared for the 20,000 people. Their old sites were cleared, while the new sites started to grow fast" (El-Kheir 1991).

Figure 2: Table of the Total and Urban Populations (000s), Sudan, 1955-2015

	1955	1973	1983	1993	2002	2008	2015[2]
Total population	10,300	14,500	21,590	25,588	31,341	39,154	37,418
Urban population	854	2,606	4,154	6,275	10,074	13,268	12,662
Urban %	8.8	18.5	20.5	25.2	33.1	29.51	33.8

Source: Adapted from 2008 Census 2009: 49; Eltayeb 2003: 1, and UN: World Urbanization Prospect 2012.

In the 1960s, the industrial zone located in Khartoum North grew rapidly. There was a strong Sudanese belief in modernization theory after independence in 1956; there was hope that through governmental-led industrial and agricultural schemes, the country would quickly develop. This encouraged diverse small-scale industrial projects[3] to set up on the industrial zone, which attracted many migrants from all over the country, including southern and western Sudanese unskilled migrants who squatted on the edges of the industrial area. "The first signs of the emergence of squatter areas in the Three Towns came with the establishment of Khartoum North Industrial Area in the early 1960s. In 1962, not more than 100 people who worked in the newly established industrial area found residence in a few huts east of the industrial area. These were obviously followed by other workers and by newcomers to the industrial area… It was not long, however, before another area emerged on the western side of the industrial area just north of El Safia town and a third one near Kober" (Elias 1972: 215). However, nearby urban settlers were frustrated with this squatting, because they assumed that this land was their own property, and subsequently they placed significant pressure on the local

[2] The decline of the total and urban population comes as a logical consequence of South Sudan secession, but the figures projected by UN agency and the Sudan National Bureau of Statistics far from being consistent, due to the lack of any reliable population Census conducted after the split of the two countries.

[3] Mainly textiles and garments, food processing and building materials.

government to act. Eventually, the government decided to forcibly removed the squatter settlers, forcing them to move to the south-eastern periphery of the city in 1971, about 15 km from the industrial zone, in an empty area near to a nomad's village called Haj Yousif. The new planned shantytown comprised four quarters beside a market and wide open space. Unfortunately, not all the inhabitants of the squatter settlement were able to secure a piece of land in the new site. For this reason, many of them ended up living on the edges of the new planned shantytown, creating a new squatter settlement. The new site subsequently became attractive to all newcomers from Western and Southern Sudan, besides all forcibly re-located people from all around the capital. These dramatic increases in the population enforced the government to upgrade more squatter settlements to become planned areas, adding four more quarters in 1974 and then further quarters in the early 1980s. The last such expansion was in 1992, when the government decided to upgrade more areas, one of which was Al-Baraka (the research area).

1.3 Urban Life

Social anthropologists have conducted most of the detailed studies of urbanization and urbanism in Africa to date. The Rhodes-Livingstone Institute in 1937, which later became known as the 'Manchester School of African Urbanism', conducted several studies and publications about the urbanization in central Africa (Copperbelt towns). The main theory used by Manchester School anthropologists was the 'equilibrium', which is the fundamental assumption of functionalism theory (Hannerz 1980).

According to Epstein (1967), every African urban-dweller tends to be involved in a complex network of social relations, comprising ties with neighbors, work-mates, friends and acquaintances. However, at the core of the network are those who fit into the flexible categories of kinship and those who count as fellow tribesmen.

Mitchell also refers to what has been variously termed as 'urban tribalism', 'supertribalism' or 'ethnicity'. This is the prevalent feature of African urbanism, as a phenomenon of a quite different order from the 'tribalism' of the rural areas.

The contributions of Mitchell, Gluckman and Epstein demonstrated that the African workers in Copperbelt mining towns still maintained their tribal identities, although their involvement in various industrial activities allowed them to establish new sets of relations. Eventually, urban-based social institutions and ties became more relevant to the African workers through establishing urban associations and trade unions. However, this analysis emphasized that African workers were largely able to switch between the 'tribal set' of behaviors and the 'urban set' of norms, through selecting their behaviors according to each specific situation of interaction and evaluating the actors involved in the interaction. The theoretical principle underlying this analysis was termed 'situational selection'. Furthermore, "in certain respects 'situational analysis' marked an important departure from the classic structuralist approach identified with Radcliffe-Brown. Certainly, situations were studied with a view to elucidating the structural principles that operated not simply in the particular situations being observed but also in wider social contexts. The divergence is more clearly to be seen in the position given to the individual" (Epstein 1992: xxv).

The most important early contribution is Philip Mayer's study of African Bantu-speaking migrants to East London town in South Africa (Mayer 1971). He distinguished vividly between the townsmen and countrymen ways of life, as well as further distinguishing between the Red Xhosa and School Xhosa within the category of country-bred Xhosa. The first group of migrants were characterized by "a 'tribal' type of moral conformism, stressing the superiority of the original undiversified institution; such institution make for multiple relations and the close-knit type of network; and this again makes for consistent moral pressure and conservatism. The processes are two-way or circular ones. It is by refusing to branch out into new habits that Red migrants retain a basis for close-knit networks; while it is by keeping the networks close-knit that they inhibit cultural branching-out" (Mayer, 1971: 292). The other category was the School Xhosa, who primarily opted for the adoption of a lifestyle similar to the "White people's ways" (Mayer, 1971: viii). For this reason, the main "characteristic of school migrants, we find a culture which has been more tolerant in principle of the engagement in diversified institutions; accordingly, a tendency towards the single—strand type of relation and the loose-knit type of network. Again this produces two—way or circular effects. Cultural specialization makes for looser-knit networks, while the looseness of the network allows for cultural specialization. The School culture, with its institutional diversification, thus carries within itself its own dynamic of change in the migrant situation" (Mayer, 1971: 292). This study shed light on the kind of structural organization that usually evolves in the newly established migrant's communities in an urban environment, and to a certain extent resembles the kind of social structure that exists in Al-Baraka community (see Chapter Three), in which the differentiation between first generation and educated people is characterized by the same principles of Xhosa migrants. Moreover, within the first generation social group, the variation between the economic migrants and the forced migrants (see Chapter Four) has many similar characteristics to the Red Xhosa and the freelance Red Xhosa who chose to have Red friends regardless of their home origin in East London in the 1950s.

In Sudan, there have been two dominant schools of urbanization theory among the urban sociological and anthropological studies (Salih 1989: 78), namely:

1—Structural functionalism theory, applied mostly by Western scholars during 1960-1970, mainly focused on the processes of urbanization and rural/urban transformations. They studied a wide range of issues related to themes such as the impact of rural/urban migration on social change, the economic and social status of migrant laborers, the emergence of new cultural entities due to population density, and rural/urban relations and linkages. For example, the research of Wendy James conducted during 1964-1965, entitled *The Shanty Towns of Port Sudan* (1980), revealed that the establishment of squatter settlements in Port Sudan city was a result of the migration of the Beja and Khasa pastoralists and the overflow of relatively wealthy town folk, who preferred to live in the quieter edges of the town rather than the overcrowded center.

2—Marxist and New-Marxist theory: this approach dominated in the 1970-1980 period in response to the rise of New-Marxist theory in Africa and Latin America. It focused on many issues, including the dynamics of rural/urban interaction and the exploitative role of urban centers as hubs for accumulating wealth from the countryside, the political economy of housing, squatter settlements and the urban land market.

Studies of squatter settlements and shantytowns under New-Marxists theory differed from their predecessors. They held that the development of squatter settlements and shantytowns was a popular response to rapid urbanization in countries that cannot or will not afford to provide services for the increasing urban population, due to the exploitive nature of the capitalist system (Zahir 1972: 222).

Following these major theoretical areas of Sudan academia, Internally Displaced Persons (IDPs) and refugee studies are almost a new research area, although recently there has been increasing interest in this area (Nilsson 2000: 27).

1.4 Ethnicity and Identity

Ethnicity grabbed the attention of social scientists in the late 1960s (Cerroni-Long 2007). The main reason was the appearance of new theories and concepts such as ethnicity instead of tribalism, and the invention of the 'ethnic boundaries' concept, conceptualized by Fredrik Barth, which led to the replacement of the idea of 'cultural difference' (Barth 1970) and the introduction of the situational/circumstantialist approach.

Ethnicity studies tend to investigate the patterns and dynamics of interaction that link groups (Sanders 2002). In particular, they focus on the locations of cross-group interactions in terms of social space rather than as physical places, wherein the cross-group interactions take place are the social boundaries between groups. The social ethnic networks and their social capital are central to the study of ethnicity in plural societies, because powerful ethnic networks are effective in expanding the employment opportunities of group members through an urban labor market.

Briefly, the theoretical positions of ethnicity studies as outlined by Eriksen (1993) are naturalist/circumstantialist (Fredrik Barth), structural functionalism (Abner Cohen), mentalist (Arnold Epstein), constructivist (Roosens, Chapman et al.) and historical (Comaroff, Peel).

The many contributions on ethnicity studies in Africa, often influenced strongly by Barth, broadly involve "a shift away from discussions of the content of ethnic identity through considerations of ethnic markers such as dress, food, language, and so on, towards a consideration of the boundaries that marks the limits of such contents. With regard to such boundaries he makes two salient points. First, that boundaries persist despite a flow of personnel and information across them; secondly—as a corollary to the first—that such groups cannot exist in isolation but only in contrast to other such groups" (Banks 1996: 12). In Sudan, Barth's theory influenced many, for example Abdul-Jalil (1985), who adopted the situational approach in his study of the ethnic identification among the Dor community in Northern Darfur: Abdul-Jalil referred to the different levels of ethnicity, e.g. national, regional and local, and argued that four main criteria can be used as indicators for the identification of ethnic groups, namely territorial, occupational, linguistic and genealogical.

A different approach was adopted by Assal (2006), who stressed resource-based conflicts taking place at the local community level, which were later transformed to ethnical identity conflicts through binary oppositions, e.g. Arabs vs. Africans, Christians vs. Muslims, North vs. South, etc. In his study of Lafofa people, Leif Manger (1994) used many similar concepts, such as Arabization, Islamization, Commercialization and Modernization, to analyze the process of social change in Lafofa, and the Nuba Mountains in general. Another contribution in this respect comes from Francis M. Deng (2005), who stressed that the identities currently in conflict in Sudan are the result of a historical legacy characterized by an institutionalized form of slavery that classified groups into a superior race of masters and inferior enslaved people. Another similar contribution is by Mukhtar (2005), who not only stressed that Sudan is in a state of crisis of national identity between two main identities in the country, North and South, but also focused on the conflict 'within' Northern identity. He divided this into an internal duality characterizing the North self-divide (black Arabs of Sudan vs. original Arabs of Arabic peninsula), which underlies the external duality characterizing the North/South divide.

The last example of this use of binary identity politics is from Makris, who studied the spirit possession cult called *tumbura* spread in surrounding shantytowns of North Khartoum (Makris 1996). He stressed that these *Zar* cult ceremonies demonstrate the contested space between the cult's devotees (the majority of whom are descendants of nineteenth-century African slaves) and Arab Muslim northerners. He also addressed the changes after the shantytowns were populated by the displaced people from Southern Sudan, whereby the Southern displaced people enabled the slave descendants to move away from the margins of the society and closer to their previous Arab masters. In his view, this movement triggered a process of identity transformation that has reflected upon the popularity of *tumbura*, which has started to rapidly decline.

1.5 Slums and Shantytowns[4] in the Global South

Many aspects of town planning in Africa have been shaped by ideology and not by objective science or a genuine desire to promote development. Njoh (2009: 9) suggests four main ideologies that shaped the planning of African cities: indigenous elitism (pre-colonial era-1884); European racism (colonial era, 1884-1960s); modernism (1960-1980s); and globalism (1990s-present). Aside from indigenous elitism, all the ideologies are alien to Africa (ibid. 2009: 17). Whereas modernism was reflected in high-

---

[4] I prefer to use the term shantytown in reference to the area under study, because it is a self-built area, and its inhabitants continue to develop the site to match the conventional standards of neighboring urban settlements, while the term "slum is usually associated with a housing area in degeneration" (Schlyter 1980: 19).

ly subsidized public housing projects, globalism led to the withdrawal of the government and entering of international development agencies and non-governmental organizations (NGOs).

Mike Davis's book *Planet of Slums* (Davis 2006) is one of the most important references for this process. He reviewed the most significant approaches and policies dealing with the three actors: slum population, governments and the international donors. Davis argues that the financial regulations that the International Monetary Fund (IMF) and the World Bank imposed on developing countries led to agricultural deregulation and financial discipline, which in turn pushed huge numbers of rural laborers to urban slums, even as cities ceased to create new jobs. He blames the growing dependence of states upon international donors and international NGOs (INGOs), which indulged a sites-and-services provision of basic infrastructure to help rationalize and upgrade self-help housing. This approach was influenced by the ideas of the English architect John Turner, who considered the people as experts of their own situations and held that they should be given the 'freedom to build' and design their neighborhoods according to their needs. The purpose was to make housing affordable to low-income households without the payment of subsidies, in contrast to the heavily subsidized public housing approach. The international finance institutions pushed for this amidst great propaganda about "helping the poor help themselves" (Davis 2006: 75). According to Davis, this approach paved the way for a withdrawal of state and local government support for slum dwellers, leaving them subject to market fluctuations. At the same time, national elites used their power to create patterns of land use and population density, which repeated older logics of colonial oppression and racial dominance. These post-colonial elites inherited and reproduced the physical footprints of segregated colonial cities. Despite the rhetoric of national liberation and social justice, they aggressively adapted the racial zoning of the colonial periods to defend their own class privileges and spatial exclusivity. The poor rural population replaced the former natives of the colonies (ibid. 2006: 96). Davis concludes by asserting "the root cause of urban slumming seems to lie not in urban poverty but in urban wealth" (Davis 2006: 95-96).

The issue of government-local people relations in worldwide slums was the focus of a significant report written by the UN Agency for Human Settlement (UN Human Settlement Program 2003). In this first global assessment of slums, the global number of slum dwellers was projected to increase to about two billion by 2020. While only 924 million people lived in slums in 2001, about 43 percent of them were living in the developing world. The report praises governmental approaches in dealing with slums, describing them as shifting away from negative policies such as forced eviction, neglect and involuntary resettlement to more positive policies such as self-help and upgrading, facilitating and rights-based policies (ibid. xxv-xxvi). The report suggested that informal settlements, where most of the urban poor in developing countries live, are increasingly seen by public decision-makers as places of opportunity, as "slums of hope" rather than "slums of despair" (ibid. xxvi). Furthermore, the report stressed that to meet the challenge of slums, urban development policies should address the issue of livelihoods of slum dwellers and urban poverty in general, thus extending beyond traditional approaches that have tended to concentrate on improving housing, infrastructure and physical environmental conditions (ibid. xxvii).

The case of Al-Baraka community reveals that these three agents in Sudan (local people, government and UN agencies/NGOs) differ in the manner and purpose through which they provide services to the shantytown's people. These differences are the result of the diverse perceptions and understandings of the character of local people and the nature of the area. Local people's perceptions and priorities about services are heavily influenced by their backgrounds and ideology, specifically their rural background and urban aspirations. At the same time, the government officials' perceptions arise from their middle-class background and their living in other parts of the city; NGOs' concerns are motivated by their Western experiences of humanitarian work, which influences their design and funding of services and development projects.

The efforts and ideologies of the agents providing the respective social services limit the alternatives of local people to satisfy their needs. The differences between the urban and rural lifestyles of local people also widen the gap between the inhabitants of Al-Baraka shantytown. As this case study shows, local settlers are working hard and passionately to achieve their respective objectives, collecting and directing all their resources towards their most important aims, while other actors, UN agencies, NGOs and the government are clearly influenced by their respective ideologies in setting very different objectives. Even if those objectives help to promote the wellbeing of local residents, the perceptions and viewpoints of local people still need to be addressed and considered. This lack of consideration has led to failed projects initiated by NGOs and the government in the Al-Baraka shantytown.[5]

1.6 Methodology

This research is essentially an ethnographic study. Accordingly, I used participant observation as the main method to collect empirical data. I rented two houses in different quarters (Nos. 2 and 4), each for six months (April-September 2010 and October 2011-March 2012 respectively), and tried to follow the daily life, activities and events of different groups and individuals living in those areas. I also used unstructured interviews, group discussions, audio records, reports, photography, genealogies, social networks diagrams and academic literature. Analysis of the data is based upon extensive listening to and transcribing of the interviews and group discussions, besides depending upon field notes. I used these resources to develop the main concepts and categories of the study. In later stages, I used the concepts of lifestyle and of localization process as the basic analytic tools to develop theoretical models that could be applied in other comparable communities in Africa. These theoretical models (Chapters Three and Seven) were supported by extensive verification methods from the first-hand data collected from the field, and literature from anthropological studies and other various disciplines.

The study used a grounded theory approach to analyze and interpret the phenomena under research, and subsequently to build a theoretical framework that is close to and illustrates the real life experiences of the people. I opted to use grounded theory because "the development of theoretically informed interpretation is the most powerful way of bring reality to light. Building theory, by its very nature, implies interpreting data, for the data must be conceptualized and the concepts related to form a theoretical rendition of reality.... Researchers concerned with building theory also believe that theories represent the most systematic way of building, synthesizing, and integrating scientific knowledge" (Strauss and Corbin 1990: 23). Therefore the research findings constitute a theoretically informed formulation of the reality under investigation. Through

[5] For more details see Bakhit (2013): From Illegal Squatter Settlement towards Legal Shantytowns: Negotiations of power and responsibilities in Khartoum shantytowns". In: *BIGSASworks!* 11: 7-21.
Also available online on: https://epub.unibayreuth.de/113/1/BIGSASworks_4_05oct 2013.pdf

this methodology, the concepts and relationships within the data are not only generated but are also provisionally tested and verified.

During this research, I realized that there were significant challenges to both collecting and analyzing data. This stemmed from the specific nature of the community under study, and the specific quality of the researcher (e.g. from same country, educated, male), besides practical considerations of the fieldwork conditions (e.g. specific times, limited resources). All this prompted the question of the extent to which the data generated could be considered representative of the whole shantytown and all segments of the population. In relation to this issue, three main challenges emerged:

1—Bias towards educated people: because they are assumed to be the voice of the community, educated residents usually deal with the government, NGOs, journalists and researchers. Moreover, they are more cooperative and willing to answer the questions in a research-appropriate and experienced manner. I solved this problem by living in different neighborhoods, which allowed me to have contacts with many other groups, like the second generation of residents, through their presence in *al-muhatta*, a hangout place for young people, which was located near my house. In addition, I followed social occasions in the neighborhoods (marriages, funerals, Ramadan breakfasts), as well as worship gatherings, where the first generation dominate. This reflected an effort to diversify my perspective.

2—Gender bias: this stems from the fact that I am a man dealing with a community dominated by men, especially in the first fieldwork trip. To solve this problem, I hired a female research assistant to conduct interviews with women inside their homes, although she conducted the interviews in the manner of a questionnaire, with very little extraneous informal conversation. In the second fieldwork period, one of my key informants was a woman working in the local committee, through whom I managed to conduct many interviews with women, discovering many aspects of women's perceptions about life. Furthermore, I recommend having more research conducted by the female researcher to grasp the complexities of women's worldview and identify the main differences with the male perceptions (Abusharaf 2009).

3—Events bias: one of the most important methods of collecting data for this study was through following events. While I mainly managed to do so during my presence in the two field periods, I also missed some important other events, such as the time of the referendum for Southern people about the future of South Sudan. My second fieldwork started a few months after the referendum in January 2011, when about two-thirds of the Southern people had already left the area for their new nation.

The process of conducting fieldwork is critical to the analysis of this thesis; traditionally most ethnographic accounts have revealed very little information concerning the actual processes of fieldwork. However, postmodernists argue that this process is crucial in the formation of ethnographic studies, stressing that anthropologists can never be unbiased observers of all that goes on in a specific field study. Fieldworkers would be present in specific places during specific periods, and consequently, they might see some things and miss others. The particular conditions of fieldwork, the socio-economic context in which it occurs, the researcher's preferences and taste, and the people seen by chance or plan, all influence and shape the resulting understanding of the community. However, ethnographic accounts have consistently been written as if the anthropologists were unbiased, omniscient observers, and this is only recently being challenged (McGee 1996: 481).

In this study, attention has been devoted to not falling into the same trap. I argue that this can be somewhat achieved by using reflexivity, in which the process of collecting and analyzing the data should be presented in a transparent way and be self-critical throughout. This thesis emphasizes that all my research data and the analysis generated from it by no means represents the whole community of Al-Baraka, but rather it strongly represents my personal experiences through fieldwork with some segments of the population of Al-Baraka community, at specific periods of time. Nonetheless, I argue that the research and its scientific findings still represent a contribution to the knowledge about identity construction in Sudanese shantytowns and many other comparable communities in other parts of the global South.

Figure 3:

IG.(3) CLASSIFICATION OF RESIDENTIAL AREAS IN GREATER KHARTOUM

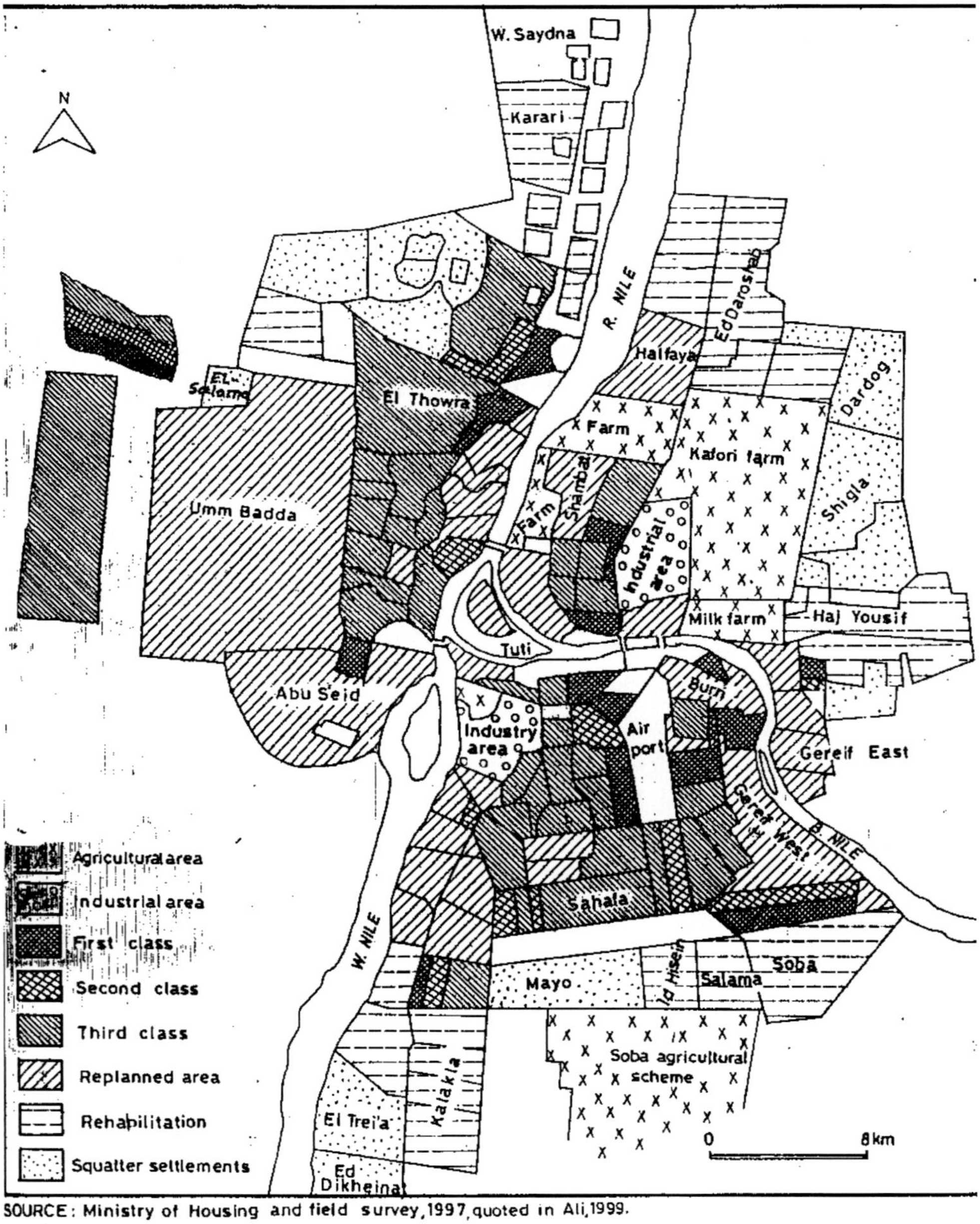

SOURCE: Ministry of Housing and field survey, 1997, quoted in Ali, 1999.

Chapter Two: Exclusion and Inclusion in Khartoum City

2.1 Introduction

Local government policies in Khartoum towards shantytowns reveal a mixture of motives and contradictory outcomes. Attempts to physically change the shantytown to comply with standards of a modern city have ended up transforming the shantytowns into fourth-class areas, marking a change from illegal squatter settlements to poor urban areas (see Figure No. 3).

The policies of the local government are driven by the urban northern Sudanese middle-class way of life and its desire to impose an Arabic-Islamic identity. "Seen from the perspective of the savanna regions of Kordofan, not only does the Nile Valley represent the economic and political centre of the country, but it also claims cultural hegemony. A specific worldview and lifestyle—i.e. a cultural orientation—emanates from this area into the hinterland. This cultural orientation is claimed by the dominant classes to be bindingly Islamic and the embodiment of a modern Arab-Sudanese identity" (Beck 1998: 254-55). This hegemonic identity is maintained and promoted mainly by educated elites from northern Sudan, and supported by businessmen. But the assimilation of the shantytown dwellers into an Arabic-Islamic identity perpetuated their low status; the acquisition of a high position in the Islamic-Arabic hierarchy of Sudan is difficult if not impossible, given that it largely depends on fictional genealogy (i.e. having presumed Arab ancestors). The historical ethnic categorizations of urban settlements are perpetuated through enforced 'acculturation,' putting shantytown settlers at the bottom of the urban hierarchy.

When the first generations of migrants/displaced settled in Al-Baraka, they encountered a new environment and different social setting to their own home environment and ways of life. The city exerts significant pressure upon these people to change their way of life to be more sympathetic to the urban northern Sudanese way of life. Thus issues of legality, physical planning, social services, and education are at the heart of the assimilation processes enforced upon these migrant people by the urban local governments and the rest of the city population.

Shantytown people encounters with the state and other urban residents are more complex than a one-way process of assimilation. It includes the shantytown people's own experience, the kind of knowledge they bring with them from their home areas, and their self-organization in their immediate environment on the peripheries of the city. It is important to gain a clear understanding of the nature of the challenges that Al-Baraka people have encountered if we want to understand how their own self-perception, definition, lifestyle and ultimately their identity, have been changed.

The first question that I started with in my analysis of my data, gathered through 12 months in the field, is what differences exist between shantytowns and the rest of the city, or what is unique about shantytowns that is worth 'researching'. Evidently, shantytowns are the poorest parts of the city economically, as well as most deprived parts in terms of services, but what are the variables creating such disparities? Certainly there are structural disparity within the Sudanese urban settlements that well documented "there are three types of settlement patterns in Sudanese towns: old towns, squatter settlements, and extensions or new areas. Each of these major sections or areas displays special characteristics" (el Dawi 1972: 246). Furthermore, through reading the history of the area and investigating the life cycles of individuals and groups in Al-Baraka, besides inferring the perceptions and the actions of people since their arrival, I settled on three variables as the main causes of differences in the shantytown settlements compared to the rest of Khartoum city.

2.2 Different Environment and Livelihood

The first challenge for shantytown settlers was to deal with a new urban environment, which was varied in comparison to their previous experience in agricultural or pastoral home areas. It must be borne in mind that the majority of migrants came to the capital as displaced people, fleeing from war, drought and desertification; at least 2.4 million people were affected by famine by mid-1985 in the western regions of the Sudan, and about 1.3 million persons, most of them children and women, experienced severe malnutrition (Eltigani 1995: 1-2). Around the same time, the civil war that broke out in the South in mid-1983 displaced about 4 million people, 1.5 million of whom ended up in the capital (Nilsson 2000: 9).

When these populations reached the capital, they found that the situation was no less difficult than in their home areas, other than their physical security: at the time of mass migration, the capital was in deep economic recession, in which less than 30 percent of industrial capacity was being used—with industrial labor the main source of jobs for rural migrants—as well as inflation and declining real wages for the rest of the city's population. Long queues for obtaining bread and food riots were frequent, coinciding with the inability of municipalities and local government councils to provide basic services due to budget cuts (Akoy 1994: 13-14).

Not all residents of the shantytowns were IDPs affected by conflicts and famines in Western and Southern regions of Sudan. Others had settled earlier in the city since the 1960s. In 1971, about 20,000 poor migrants were evacuated from the industrial zone to Haj Yousif in the outskirts of the capital, where 3,000 plots were distributed, and the area named Wehda el Wataniya. Eventually, the Al-Baraka area emerged on the edges of this legal shantytown, where the people who could not find a plot in Wehda el Wataniya—and other newcomers—resided, until the settlement was later legalized.

This urban environment required many resources and new knowledge for migrants/displaced, who needed to change the way in which they built their homes and planned the streets. They also needed to learn how to deal with paperwork and bureaucratic procedures. Furthermore, they needed to work collectively to provide their area with basic services, besides learning different ways to protect their ownership of their new suburban homes. This was a significant community challenge, because the local government made no other options available to these local people.[6]

Evidently, these people's adaption to the new urban environment is most noticeable in the way in which people built and organized their houses. This strongly affected the planning of the area in 1992-1994, giving it a gridiron structure (see appendices), with each block composed of around 10-18 plots separated by small open spaces, and each quarter containing a large service area in the middle, with schools, markets, etc. The materials used strongly reflect the knowledge locals brought with them from their home areas, as well as the urban knowledge that they accumulated through living on the peripheries of the capital, especially the younger generations. This was particularly obvious during the rainy season.

In May and June, people in Al-Baraka usually start their preparation for the rainy season. This is noticeable as many young people work on

---

[6] A shorthand to describe non-government, non-official populations with little social capital outside of their suburbs, with menial or self-employed incomes, and often from IDP backgrounds.

repairing and renovating their rooms and outside walls, or build new rooms. They often use mud in two ways. Firstly, they make mud bricks (locally called 'green bricks') by mixing mud with sand, producing bricks using a large brick mold and leaving them on the street to dry under the sun, before subsequently using the bricks for building the rooms and walls. The rooms are usually roofed traditionally, using straw, wood, and mud mixed with dung on top. More recently, people have begun to plaster the walls of new rooms with cement mixed with sand, which gives the appearance of rooms made of red bricks. These rooms then take on the typical shape of the rooms in the middle-class areas, which are usually roofed with metal sheets (zinc), held down by red bricks.

The second use of mud is making *zibâla*, a mixture of mud, dry grass and dung, which is fermented over a few days and creates a strong bad smell. This is a traditional building material in rural areas in Western and North Sudan, but it needs annual maintenance because heavy rains damage it. Many people prepare *zibâla* simply to renovate their walls, but the use of this material is in decline because people consider it as 'traditional' and rural, and the smell of the *zibâla* is unpleasant.

There are other construction materials, such as concrete, red bricks and cement bricks, which are not specifically timed to be used in advance of the rainy season, but few houses are built with these materials. However, the use of concrete, cement and cement bricks is steadily increasing, which suggests increasingly affluent locals who want to adopt a middle-class style of building. Building therefore reflects the increasing gaps between rich and poor in the Al-Baraka area. Some residents still live in houses made of plastic sheets, tin and straw, not only on the peripheries of Al-Baraka but throughout the community, in open spaces, empty plots or buttressing houses in the street. In the plot opposite my rented house on my first fieldwork period, there was a woman living with her two children in a room made of straw, empty sacks, plastic sheets and cardboard cartons; in the evening she would sell tea in the empty space in the plot. When the weather became very hot during the day, she sat in the shade of a traditional verandah made of straw and empty sacks, locally called a *rakûba*, where passing people could see her with her children. She also had a pit latrine in the corner of the plot, separated by plastic sheets.

As with the construction of their homes, the people of Al-Baraka needed to deal with the challenges of adapting to new livelihoods; many residents had been farmers, pastoralists, or a combination of the two in their areas of origin. The only way to survive in Khartoum, for them, was to learn how to be workers in government institutions, lower ranks in the armed forces or police, or in small factories as unskilled laborers. Alternatively, they could choose to be part of the informal economy and work as small traders. The informal economy is the only economic arena in which the capacity for recruitment is unlimited, despite risks of financial stress and few opportunities for advancement; for many, though, there are often no other options. Migrants frequently switch between informal activities, with careers often dependent upon trial and error methods. When a new and profitable business opportunity opens up, large numbers of people switch to it, swamping the market and reducing profits. Recent estimates concerning the size of the informal economy in Khartoum put the figure at 45% of the working population (Pantuliano 2011: 15), although on observation it seems more than that, especially following the loss of oil revenues from the northern Sudan's national budget after the independence of South Sudan in 2011.

Women appear to be the breadwinners in many families in poor areas in the capital, engaging in several self-employment activities, particularly selling food and tea in public areas to selling local brewed alcohol called *aragi* and *marîsa.* Indeed, the brewing of local alcohol is a common livelihood activity for many formerly displaced women, and is risky work in both economic and social terms. Many women are involved in brewing, and thus competition is fierce and profits are accordingly only marginal. However, the threat of frequent police raids[7] is very real, and many of the women brewers are frequently arrested, compounding hardships for their families (Gore 1998: 190). Others opted to work in nearby agriculture projects, as in the Al-Baraka area, especially for women live in Quarters No. 2,4 owing to the proximity of their houses to the farms. Working in these nearby farms is considered the best option for women, particularly older generations, because they often have experience in agriculture in their original areas. The workday starts very early at about five o'clock in the morning, although employment is not guaranteed. The daily wage is about 15 Sudanese Pounds (SDG) (about $4.30); for many women this is not considered a bad wage, particularly as there is usually more than one person working in the household, or the woman might

[7] According to the governmental law in Khartoum selling and drinking of alcohol is prohibited, usually punished by lashes, fines and imprisonment.

have more than one source of income. Hawa Naurain[8] explained her accounting:

> "We pay for rent 70 pounds monthly, it is one room ... I take care of my children then I go to the projects (agricultural farms) to work. I work only in the projects, not permanent work, one day find and other not find works [sic]. Our father (husband) [is] not here, he gives us money only when he sends [it]. There is no fixed time to his sending [it], sometimes one month, sometimes two months, only when it comes. I consume every day about 15 pounds for foods and schools, and I obtain it all by myself, except the time when he sends to us ... In the house there are other three families [renting] part of it also, one of them my uncle... most of the time [I] am going to [a] private clinic to treat my children, it [costs] me in average about 30-35 pounds for the light medicines [sic]. ... I don't participate in any sandûq[9] even the small one, I just work and spend what I have [earned], I earn formally 10 pound for workday and [it has] now become 15 pounds, so [I] use [it] for the daily expenditure, and when the other money [comes] after one or two months, I added [it] to them. ... When I was born my child [did not have a] celebration ceremony (simâya) or coffee meeting. ... In Darfur I worked in the agriculture but here [there are] projects, there we work in agriculture and [orchards], but here [is] different... we just go and work. I got the skills of farming like weeding and picking, from the country (homeland). I learnt from my childhood; our relatives taught us from [an] early age. I choose to work in the project because I don't have other options, and I want to work, because I have commitments, all what I earn I expend in my house. I don't have any other thing by this side or that. My husband knows that am working in the project, now he doesn't know how much I earn, because they increased [it recently], but he knew earlier I earn 10 pounds in a day. I couldn't save any money, all what remains I spend in [transportation] to other social activities; but sometimes there is no work, and we just [sit] down."

For young people, working in formal jobs such as in the army or police seems preferable, especially the latter because it is enables them to have significant extra income through bribes. There are two departments of the police that are notorious in this respect: the traffic police, which people compare to working abroad in the Gulf states (I have seen many of them

---

[8] This interview was conducted by my female research assistant in Al-Baraka, 2010.

[9] Revolving money saving associations, which are usually very popular with women in Sudan.

holding extravagant mobile phones), and the Department of Public Order, which is responsible for raiding places that are making and selling locally-brewed alcohol. Another good option for work is in driving rickshaw taxis, where daily incomes might exceed 70 SDG ($20), more than the average wage of a bank employee, albeit only if the driver is the owner of the rickshaw. Many other young people prefer to work in the industrial zone in largely unskilled jobs in food processing factories. However, as one young man told me,[10] the problem is that the majority of factories do not hire permanent staff, but prefer to employ workers on a daily basis. The factory managers maintain this by asking their employees to stop working a few days before reaching the three-month threshold, after which a worker should be offered a permanent job according to employment law. Furthermore, they work seven days a week, with Friday counting as two days, at a daily wage of SDG10 ($2.50).

While young men know that the work is hard and wages are very low, many generally prefer to continue with this employment route until they find better options; often one can only obtain information about other work opportunities through going to the industrial zone. Common knowledge in the industrial zone includes the fact that the best place to work is the Coca-Cola factory, but work is not available for the whole week; the Siga wheat factory is another very good option, but you need to know someone inside the factory to find a job there. To acquire these jobs, jobseekers not only need to have some kind of education certificate, but also need to maneuver dominant local cultural barriers, such as learning a new language (i.e. urban Arabic), and for Southern and Nuba people, adapting their religious beliefs by attaching themselves to churches and abandoning their traditional religious customs. Muslims from Western Sudan who practiced Sufi Islam in their home areas are generally socially forced to move towards [11]urban Islam.

One of the strategies effectively adopted in early stages of settlement by new residents is to differentiate between home and work spaces, through keeping their home space identical to old patterns in their origi-

---

[10] Interview with Adam, 5 August 2010; he had been working in the industrial zone for a long time in different jobs. Interview conducted in Al-Baraka.

[11] Urban Islam denotes all religious practices based in urban areas and brought by different modern Islamic groups (i.e. Muslim Brotherhood, Salfi groups) and usually sponsored by the state. Although Sufi groups are also present and active in urban contexts, usually they occupy a very marginal position in terms of popularity and influence in the shantytowns.

nal areas as much as possible. This might explain why locals tend to use the same building materials, social organizations and daily activities as in their 'homelands'. However, as time goes on and they establish themselves in their urban environment, whether through their own will or by force, local's homes and private patterns tend to have more similarity with other parts of the capital city. However, they generally still organize differently in terms of their urban planning (fourth-class residences, the lowest grade in Khartoum) and housing materials. Mayer also observed these basic responses to urban challenges in his profound account of Xhosa migrants:

> "The country-bred Xhosa who migrates to East London must, as is obvious, learn another mode of living in order to accommodate himself to this very different environment; we have seen that the new mode may or may not be an urbanized one. It may involve cultural urbanization (learning a preference for urban ways and institutions) and/or structural urbanization (striking permanent roots in town), which in present conditions do not necessarily go hand in hand. But it may involve neither; some kinds of migrants, particularly Red men, have been found to stay for long years in town ('stabilization') without doing either. If some migrants become genuinely urbanized, then, there are many who resist urbanization, continuing to look on themselves as countrymen in temporary or perhaps permanent exile; and many others whose response is ambiguous, and their ultimate fate uncertain" (Mayer 1971: 283).

Shantytown residents must leave their home spaces searching for work to financially support themselves, whether in the formal or informal economy. As such they need to negotiate urban space, with its different forms and organization, controlled by others who are more powerful both materially and symbolically. As such, for shantytown residents, public spaces in other parts of the city resemble arenas of passive interactions, alien spaces belonging to powerful others, or, for some, a space for learning ideals that they need to replicate.

2.3 Being at the Bottom of the Urban Hierarchy

According to the ethnic hierarchy that prevails in the northern parts of Sudan, people from Southern Sudan and the Nuba mountains, and to a lesser extent those from Darfur, are considered as having the lowest status due to their different cultural features, such as different religions or ethnic origins. This is because the majority of people from these regions consider themselves as coming from African ethnic origins, while the majority of people in north Sudan consider themselves as coming from Arab origins. Accordingly, Ja'aliyiin, Shaygiyya, and Dangala, the main ethnic groups in the Nile Valley, have dominated the Sudanese state since the pre-colonial period, particularly since the introduction of Islam and Arabism to Sudan in the sixteenth century, accompanied by a bitter legacy of slavery. After the rise of the Funj Sultanate (1504-1820) and the Fur Kingdom, and the spread of Islam and the Arabic language in northern Sudan, the slave-raiding frontier moved further towards the south. The adoption of an Arab/Islamic identity by northern Sudanese groups became a major criterion for differentiating themselves from the non-Muslim groups of the south and other areas of Sudan. While Ja'aliyiin and Shaygiyya ethnic groups claim direct Arab origins, the Dangala still claim Nubian origins, which date back to the 5000BC period in the Nile Valley. Nonetheless, all Nubian ethnic groups are very much Arabized and have become a part of the northern elites who have dominated the Sudanese state since the country's independence. The construction of any particular identity involves the development of specific perceptions about others. The Arabized northern Sudanese thus adopted stigmatizing ethnic labels to refer to non-Muslim groups in the South. As such the slave–raiding frontier was defined and maintained in ideological, ethnic and geographical terms: the inhabitants of Dar Fertit, the Nuba Mountains and upper Blue Nile became easy targets for slave traders from northern Muslim groups (Sikainga 1996: 8).

The northern Arabized elites primarily assert their Arabic/Islamic identity "to maintain and reinforce their hegemony as a minority government but also in part because of their own identity struggle" (Pekkinen 2009: 1). The identity struggles of northern people were based on the essential problem that "there is disparity between Northerners' self-perception of their identity and others' perception of them. Northerners think of themselves as Arabs, whereas the Arabs think otherwise" (Mukhtar 2005). Indeed the deep crisis of self-identification of many northern people is clearly reflected in their views on their 'African-origin' fellow citizens, who they perceive as being subject to their domination, and as having an inferior status by virtue of being the descendants of enslaved Africans. This inferior position was maintained and extended to shantytown settlers, and consolidated by other urban factors (such as their high rate of illiteracy, poverty, and their rural background). The policy of the government concerning urban areas should also be borne in mind: older quarters and upper-middle class areas have always enjoyed the largest piece of the city's cake.

This historical and social background means that relations between shantytown dwellers and the rest of the city population have always tended to be based upon majority-minority relations. This relationship strongly reflects the hieratical system that dominates the country as a whole, where people in north and central Sudan have dominated the state, economy and national culture, and have treated other parts of the country as mere peripheries. This has created a stereotypical image of shantytown people as the most vulnerable and stigmatized segment of the population. Whenever shantytown dwellers cross invisible boundaries to other parts of Khartoum, they encounter significant barriers of enforced behavioral patterns, stigma and social values that remind them about their positions in the city ladder, and which both persuade and force them to adhere to their rural traditions and thier 'residential spaces'.

In the same line, the attitude of the government towards illegal settlements of poor people has long been informed by this ideology, in what I term as a 'demolish-legalize policy'. This policy has tended to legalize some settlements by re-planning or upgrading them, usually in remote areas, and demolishing squatter settlements located near the center and in high value areas. For example, in early 1971 the government evacuated about 29,000 inhabitants (Zahir 1972), who were mainly unskilled workers originally from Western Sudan, from the area near the industrial zone of North Khartoum. The government moved them to a new legal settlement in Wehda el Wataniya, planned as Fourth Class settlement, on the periphery of the city. In 1971, the government initially planned four quarters, with one quarter as market and another quarter as open space. However, later waves of migrants settled illegally around the market. The government added another four quarters in 1983, and a further eight quarters on the south in 1986, renaming this area Dar es Salam; these were distributed to former militia members and soldiers in national army belong to the ruling party at that time. The last upgrading was in 1992, when the government upgraded the Al-Baraka area, made up of four quarters, as well as the Karton Barona and Takamol areas.

Planners and official administrators believe that the best solution to the problem of squatter settlements is to eradicate the sites and resettle them in re-planned areas with more urban services. The contradiction here is that although there are many areas in the city not planned and legally considered as squatter settlements (e.g. old areas, nearby villages), they are mainly populated by middle class people and relatively better-off farmers from north Sudan. The authorities apply the Re-organization of Villages program in these areas as a process of legalization: "the program has effectively started six years ago. During this time more than seventy villages have been organized and sixteen subdivisions re-planned. The number of families involved in the process are about 190,000, making up an overall population of about 1.3 million people" (Bannaga 2000: 10). Those villages were connected to public services even when they were illegal squatter settlements. Additionally, the program focuses on re-opening and modifying the existing streets without any significant demolitions or evacuations of inhabitants.

In the mid-1990s, the government started re-planning the Karton Kassala (currently officially named Al-Baraka) squatter settlement, using the lowest standard of Fourth Class settlement. The main feature of a Fourth Class settlement area is one where the settlement and the buildings are considered as temporary; short term leases are given, but no building standards are required and very little or no publicly funded amenities and services are provided (Ahmed 1989: 53), with a minimum size of houses (about 217-247m²) and a minimum size of open spaces, facilities, and requirements of construction materials (see Figure No. 4). It is designed to settle as many people whilst engaging as few government services as possible.

Therefore, the planning and upgrading of squatter settlements was not intended to change the socio-economic position of the people, but rather to consolidate and legalize their position in the city as the lowest status of people. As such this policy encouraged shantytown residents to develop a distinct lifestyle that emphasizes and enhances their difference from the mainstream of the city, by keeping stronger relationships with their home areas and maintaining traditional cultures, with minimum interactions with an urban way of life. This is encouraged by physical segregation (e.g. areas planned as Fourth Class settlements, at the periphery of the city), and socio-economic marginalization (e.g. 'lowest' ethnic status, low-income jobs). However, at the same time, many people in shantytowns try to be part of the urban mainstream by reducing the scale and characteristics of their personal differences (e.g. via education, technology, and work).

Figure 4: Table of the Classifications of Legal Residential Areas in Khartoum

Land class	Minimum plot size	Minimum standards of building materials	Maximum build-up area	Width of roads
First Class	500m^2	permanent (bricks, cement, mortar)	2/3 of plot	10-40m
Second Class	400m^2	bricks, cement, mortar, gishra (outer building from permanent materials, inner building from mud bricks)	2/3 of plot	10-40m
Third Class	300m^2	gishra, jalûs (mud)	2/3 of plot	10-40m
Fourth Class	200m^2	wood, cartons, grass	—	20m

Source: Adapted from Banaga 1996: 9.

Shantytown residents broadly express their approval and support for upgrading their area, and are also satisfied with increased services from the urban authorities. However, they are also aware of their position in the urban ladder as deprived people. This is compounded by their complex relations with their middle class neighbors. The distances between their communities go beyond the physical: this includes social, economic and political distance. The planning policy clearly results in fixing and protecting the urban hierarchy by maintaining the broadly low position of shantytowns in Khartoum.

To overcome this, many local people have tried to create their own space, to the extent that shantytowns become a world in themselves. This generally happens through locals creating what can be called a 'core area'. In 1971, when the government was planning Wehda el Wataniya area, Quarter Number Three became the main market, as well as the center of transportation in the area; subsequent upgraded shantytowns emerged around this center. This center ('core area') gives the shantytowns a local hub and a kind of independence from the influence of the center of Khartoum city. People of shantytowns depend on the core area for all their commodities and services, and their leisure activities like TV and cinema clubs, traditional wrestling, cafés and traditional healing centers, all of which are organized in the market arena. At the same time, relationships with the center of the city are increasingly limited, maintained only through work, because relatives usually live in other shantytown areas around other peripheries of the city (see Figure No. 1), and transport links connect these core areas directly, avoiding the center of the city whenever possible.

The core area generally includes the oldest residents of the shantytowns; this broadly means that the core area residents have had greater opportunities to become more highly educated and wealthier, due to their market ownership and work in trades in the core area; their houses are also usually on the most valuable land in the shantytown. Although the core area is considered the center and the connecting point for the shantytown, it generally most strongly resembles middle class areas. It also has the strongest relationship with the center of the city out of the rest of the shantytown; this is explicit in the presence of local governmental institutions within the boundaries of the market.

2.4 Heterogeneity of the Local Population

The people of Al-Baraka have migrated or been displaced from different parts of Southern and Western Sudan, with little previous communication with Khartoum. This includes many small ethnic groups that have very little pre-knowledge of each other, and communities that are mutually hostile in their home areas. In a joint survey conducted by a number of INGOs[12] in 2003 covering all major shantytowns in Khartoum, it was found that "the major ethnic groups are Dinka and Nuba (representing 25.4% and 20.6% of the households respectively). Arab ethnic groups (including Misiri) make up 14% of the IDP households and Fur 13.1%. Other significant groups include; Shilluk – 4.1%, Bari – 4%, Firtit – 3.2%, Nuer – 2.3% and Funj – 2%" (CARE et al. 2003: 14). These figures indicate the diverse ethnic backgrounds of shantytown residents; it was a huge challenge for these disparate ethnic groups to live together in a new urban environment.

[12] The group included CARE, IOM (International Organization for Migration) and the UNDP (United Nations Development Programme). Their aim was to conduct a socio-economic/demographic survey of IDPs (Internally Displaced Persons) in different parts of Khartoum; the sample population consisted of 1,800 households.

For this reason, at early stages of settlement many ethnic clashes happened between local residents. Saymon notes, “at first it was not like this, before the planning there were many tribal conflicts, especially in Karton Kassala, every day you found [a] tribe clash[ed] with [another] tribe, for that we established [a] leaders council, from 36 tribes for each one leader then the conflict stopped, before the planning, they established one council [which] ceased the fighting.”[13] This hostile situation created an internal social hierarchy, where each ethnic group claimed superiority over others, strengthened by the strong presence of ethnic organizations in the area, and using these associations to gain power and privileges. However, with time, many cross-cutting institutions like schools, local committees, sport clubs, and worship gatherings started to have a more inclusive effect upon perceptions of belonging among local people. Another uniting factor was the realization that all residents had some fundamental differences to the dominant culture in Khartoum. Finally, since their arrival, residents had shared the difficulties and challenges of shantytown life, creating a common history among them: they mutually suffered from the settlement’s lack of legality, water, electricity, transportation links, and good jobs, as they were stereotyped as poor and IDPs by other residents of the city.

One way to overcome these internal divides was for the residents to widen their definitions of themselves, and incorporate new ethnic groups under the umbrella of larger ethnic groups from the area of origin. This meant that ethnicity in the shantytowns came to have different meanings and implications than understandings of ethnicity in rural home areas. If we consider all large ethnic groups in the shantytown (e.g. the Fur, ‘Southerners’, Nuba and Kalmba), none of these ethnic groups directly resemble their counterpart identities in their home lands; sometimes ‘Khartoum’ identities are non-existent in home areas, having been invented to satisfy urban needs of the local population. For example, the Fur ethnic group in Al-Baraka includes many other ethnic groups coming from Darfur, none of whom identify themselves as Fur in Darfur; they differ in many aspects in their cultural practices, they speak different languages, and believe in different history and myths about their origins. What they share with the Fur ethnic group is their subordination to the Fur during the era of the Fur Sultanate; it seems as if the dominance of

[13] Interview with Saymon, head of the popular committee of Quarter Four, and member of the legislative assembly of East Nile area; he is also a tribal leader of the Shilluk in the area. Al-Baraka, 21 March 2009.

the Fur as an ethnic unit of identification in Khartoum is a result of this history, although playing out in a very different way to residents of Darfur.

For the 'Southerners', this description simply refers to a geographical rather than ethnic entity, where all ethnic groups living in this regional space are considered part of this 'pan-ethnic' group. One of the results of this powerful designation was the formation of South Sudan as an independent country in July 2011. Southern Sudan is very diverse region, with many historical rivalries between main ethnic groups (e.g. Dinka, Nuer, and Shilluk, among many others). As Deng asserts, perpetuating the name of a Dinka person requires the collective efforts of his family to call for the cooperation of clan and tribal members, and hence places an emphasis on unity and harmony as essential ethnic values. Since this emphasis is designed to minimize dissent within the lineage, a sense of pride in the Dinka's lineage and in oneself as a dependant of that lineage becomes compulsory. Deng further stresses that the Dinka are a very proud people, singularly and collectively. Such pride is an outcome of the honor and self-respect required for maintaining an excellent name (Deng 1987). Therefore, when Southern people's interactions with the outside world increased—through many routes including migration towards the North—they were encouraged to see themselves as all 'Southern' people. Thus, it is possible to argue that the formation of the Southern Sudan identity is a result of interactions with other ethnic groups, accompanied by their implied low status by Khartoum residents and the Sudanese state, a degradation which largely takes place in urban sittings.

The same route to self-recognition can be seen among the Nuba people, who live together on one chain of hills in Sudan while having many diverse cultural divisions. They started to realize their common identity through increasing contact with the outside world, their shared histories of oppression, and of slave trade raids. When they migrated to urban areas, largely to squatter settlements, they started to employ and strengthen their shared identity by living together. Later this identity was reinforced by re-inventing parts of their traditions from the original area (e.g. Nuba wrestling). Politically, their identity was also revived by a group of educated elites aiming to resist the hegemony of the northern-run Sudanese state. It was logical to make an alliance with Southern pan-ethnic organizations under the guerilla movement the Sudanese People Liberation Movement/Army (SPLM/A) against central government authority, as they shared the same low political, economic and social status in Sudan, especially in the urban areas.

In the same line, we find the Kalmba, which includes several ethnic groups from Western Sudan; other ethnic groups describe them as people who have migrated from Chad to Sudan. In fact, many of those ethnic groups live across the border, with some segments of these ethnic groups living in Sudan, while the remainder living in Chad. Ethnic groups like the Zaghawa, Tama and Bargo might be included in Kalmba ethnic group, while other ethnic groups portray them as isolated ethnic groups; in fact, many of them have strong contacts with their neighbors, and they often participate in and dominate the informal sector in the central market.

2.5 Historical Development of Al-Baraka Area

2.5.1 The stage of squatter settlement

The first stage of the Al-Baraka squatter settlement stretched from 1970 to the re-planning of the area in 1992. People lived based on ethnic enclaves, whereby each ethnic group had its neighborhood ruled by an ethnic group leader titled *Sultan*, some of whom were appointed by local people and approved by their chiefs in the areas of origin, while others were appointed by themselves or only by their close relatives. This depended on whether the system of the respective ethnic group was centralized, such as the Shilluk, or segmentary, like the Dinka.[14]

Throughout this period, relations between ethnic enclaves were characterized by tensions and clashes, which were partially solved after the formation of a tribal leaders' council. This council also dealt with disputes between individuals of different ethnic backgrounds. NGOs and the people themselves provided services and security. Many UN agencies, INGOs and NGOs worked in the area when it was a squatter settlement, including UNHCR, UNICEF, ADRA, Dawa Islamiyya, Save the Children, Sudanese Council of Churches, CRS and CARE. Various INGOs provided health centers, water wells and food assistance. The people themselves organized security, albeit in a rather chaotic way, which gave the area a reputation for criminality. Karton Kassala—the former name of the area—was associated with drug dealing, illegal local alcohol distribution, prostitution and theft. This might have been one reason for the eagerness of the local people to plan and legalize their settlement. To make

[14] Interview with Sultan William, Al-Baraka, 15 August 2010.

matters worse, the government took a destructive role in the squatter settlement, considering it illegal; indeed, on several occasions the government destroyed whole areas in pursuing what can be called its 'demolish-legalize' policy. This policy always tended towards legalizing some settlements by planning or upgrading them, usually in remote areas, and demolishing the squatter settlements located near the center or in real estate areas of high value. Much evidence in Khartoum shows that the local urban government exerts direct authoritarian pressure on the location of displaced persons and shantytown settlers in the conurbation by demarcating specific locations where they can set up homes (e.g. Dar es Salam, created towards the end of the 1980s, and four camps for displaced persons, which were set up in 1991), as well as through brutal mass evacuation actions and the formation of resettlement areas for these population groups that have been moved out of the city (de Geoffroy 2009: 514).

In 1988, floods and heavy rains inundated the capital, causing wide-ranging destruction of the shantytowns, since they were constructed of only mud and cardboard. As is usual in such disasters, the poorer sections of society suffered most. These people tended to live in mud houses and 82% of the damaged and destroyed houses were built of such materials (Davies & Walsh 1997: 124). The affected people from Karton Kassala and nearby squatter settlements moved to a nearby new market and took shelter in its empty shops. Meanwhile, the government, as represented by the Prime Minister, refused to visit the area,[15] unlike other nearby legal shantytowns, because it was not legally considered a part of the city. Eventually, after a few years the government acknowledged the problem and re-planned Karton Kassala and other nearby squatter settlements.

2.5.2 The planning stage

Initial contact between local people and the government was established during this phase, implying the government's recognition of the shantytown residents as part of the capital city. Locals agreed to participate effectively in the planning measures, because they had observed the benefit of planning in neighboring areas. This participation included the selection of local experts who helped the planning bureaucrats directly, as well as local committees who contributed by informing the whole community about the procedure of legalizing their homes. The bureaucratic procedures of legalizing land ownership included several steps, such as registration, investigation, providing documents, and paying fees.

[15] Interview with Saymon Ushan Ding, Al-Baraka, 21 March 2009.

However, the procedures of gaining ownership of the houses during the legalization of settlements were very expensive and there were fees for registering the ownership of the house. It was not possible to exempt any owner of a house from paying the fees unless by permission from the minister of urban planning, which was difficult to obtain.[16] Nonetheless, it represented a first step towards integrating the residents in city life, a style of life characterized—as many expressed—by placing more trust in 'paperwork' than 'informal (verbal) agreements'.

Prolonged negotiations took place between local committees and the government about how many families had the right to settle in the area, and subsequently about the size of each house. In the Sudanese context, houses are usually sizable, with 200m^2 as a minimum for formal housing due to hot weather, gender segregation and the plentiful availability of land (see Figure No. 4). In the various quarters, significant differences exist between the sizes of houses. Quarter Number Two has the smallest allocated space per house (217m^2), because the majority of inhabitants were from the same ethnic group (Fur) and wanted as many people as possible to settle together, and not be dispersed to other quarters. The planning authority was evidently mainly concerned with re-structuring the area to be more organized physically, meaning that they did not intervene in the makeup of the population or its distribution during the negotiations. Instead, they left those issues in the hands of the local committees and the residents, which gave the local population a sense of participation, and local committees the feeling of being decision-makers rather than merely recipients.

The planning stage lasted for about two years (1992-1994), during which local committees and planning officials, assisted by local experts, proposed new streets and open spaces. This necessitated forcibly evacuating 'non-eligible' inhabitants and relocating other eligible settlers to new houses. It was the first real interaction between the two agents, in an interaction that included negotiations and the sharing of responsibilities; indeed, it was the first time the local people felt that their collective agency could make a difference.

The planning stage required the inclusion of shantytown people in the formal city boundaries in official or legal terms. However, it was clear that the balance of power remained in favor of the government. In effect, planning gave legality to shantytown settlements but preserved the

16 Interview with Khamis, a former local expert for the planning authority, Al-Baraka, 28 May 2010.

status quo hierarchy of the urban setting. In fact, the planning stage embedded the low status of shantytown residents as institutionalized "Fourth Class areas" (Ahmad 1989: 53).

2.5.3 The stage of planned settlement

When the planning stage was over, a new reality began to emerge. The local committees became the official representatives of local people, not only due to their role in planning, but also in providing much-needed services such as water and electricity. Accordingly, the position of tribal leaders was weakened; their role was restricted to familial issues, and even this depended on the acquiescence of the individuals.

In 2008, the population in Al-Baraka stood at about 38,580 people (Republic of Sudan Central Bureau of Statistics 2008), which represented about 75.5% of the total population of Al-Baraka according to the National Census of 1993 (Merghani 1998: 19-20). This population decline is a direct result of the upgrading of the area since 1994. However, shantytowns remain the most densely populated areas in the city, largely because they generally accommodate more than one family per house due to the low-income jobs available to inhabitants. While statistics show that the average number of household in Al-Baraka is 6.5 members (CARE and IOM 2003), sometimes three households share one house.

Whereas NGOs used to run development projects and services in shantytowns during the 1980s, after the deterioration of diplomatic relations between the Sudanese government and Western countries the role of the NGOs diminished considerably as the government accused Western-based NGOs of implementing foreign agendas. This was largely a product of the Arabic-Islamic ideology of the government after the Islamic movement party took power in 1989. Remarkably, the first action initiated by the government after planning was to change the name of the area to 'Al-Baraka', an Islamic name denoting 'holy blessing' in Arabic, which is generally used in religious contexts. This clearly illustrates the government's vision for the area.

Meanwhile, people intensified relations with nearby legal shantytowns, and especially with the central market or the 'core area'; impressive permanent houses appeared and shops were packed with a range of goods. A huge change came with the introduction of electricity in 2007, when people had their first taste of modernized urban life, with an enormous array of electronic devices becoming accessible. Previously, people had used private generators for lighting at night.

All ten schools of the area were transferred into the management of the government, apart from one that belonged to the Catholic Church. Besides these, a growing number of private schools sprang up, run by the educated young generation. Other members of this young generation born and raised in the area started to engage in economic activities within and outside the area, such as driving rickshaws. Meanwhile, large numbers of their peers were working in government institutions in the lower ranks, the police service and the army. While some NGOs continued their efforts in the field of healthcare, as there was no government-funded medical center in the area, some supported small developmental programs through local partners. They had permission to continue because they were allied with the government, such as Islamic NGOs, or agreed to work with community-based organizations (CBOs) through local partners.

In this chapter, I explained in a detailed way how the variables of different environments and livelihoods, being at the bottom of urban hierarchy, as well as the heterogeneity of local population of the shantytowns, play crucial roles in differentiating shantytown residents and areas from the rest of the Khartoum urban population. I also explained how the local government, through its consistent urban policies, has consolidated the gap between the marginalized shantytown populations and other wealthier parts of the city.

To understand how this critical position of the shantytown influences local people, and in what ways they are able to respond and engage with this, in the coming chapter I will try to detail the social structure of Al-Baraka community. This section aims to document the manner in which local people have been responding to the challenge of being at the bottom of the urban hierarchy, and also to understand how the local community are responding to the wider multiple contexts of their existence, which, beside the impact of other parts of the city, also includes the original areas of the first generation and the global connections made available through the media and technology.

Chapter Three: The Social Structure of Al-Baraka

3.1 Introduction

This chapter will focus on the social structure of Al-Baraka community. Firstly, I will try to explore how the concept of 'lifestyle' might be useful in identifying important features of the social structure of Al-Baraka community, as well as how it enables us to unpick the local classifications of different lifestyle groups. This is not only through oral accounts, but also through observations of normal daily activities and specific social practices, including three particular components: materiality, competence and meaning. It is possible to observe and measure lifestyle practices through a participant observation method, while the concept of identity seems more vague and difficult to trace empirically. The importance of the lifestyle concept lies in its ability to reflect the reality of social life empirically as well as theoretically, for which I will use the concept of social practice. This will be followed by examining the concept of ethnic identity in shantytowns, including how people tend to use the idea, and the kinds of difference that exist between the practices of ethnic organizations in locals' home areas compared with Al-Baraka.

I will discuss in detail the three distinct lifestyles that exist in Al-Baraka, and their relationships to each other. Through using a triangular diagram as a visual aide, I will try to show the complexity of relations between the three lifestyles, and how people practically manage their choices. Furthermore, I will try to explain how different personal positions in the triangle might result in different sets of behaviors and practices within the same lifestyle group, or with other groups in the corners of the triangle. The triangular represents the theoretical model that I developed from the case of Al-Baraka community; I would infer that it is also applicable to other shantytowns in Sudan, and that it is a relevant model for further comparison studies in other African shantytowns.

I started analyzing the data, collected during the two fieldwork periods, by asking the broad general question: how do people in Al-Baraka define themselves and others?

It was obvious that local residents have generally been using their ethnic identification as the main method to distinguish between themselves, as individuals or groups. In the field, I was soon informed that the majority of population in Quarter No. 1 are Nuba and Fur people, in Quarter No. 2 there are Fur people, and in Quarters No. 3, 4 are the

Southern people. I was informed that the person whose house I rented is from the Bargo tribe, although other people assumed that he came from Chad. It was not unusual to hear someone call another person by his own ethnic group, given that it is a source of pride for everyone.

The justification offered by elders about using ethnic groups as a way of identification is that it resembles what people used to practice in their home areas. Others consider it as a kind of refusal to be assimilated to the way of life of other parts of the city; indeed, it is also an instrument to keep people together, to help each other at times of need. However, if we compare the nature of the ethnic groups in the shantytowns and in the areas from which they originally come—as we will do later—it is easy to conclude that vast differences still exist. This indicates that, for any member of the shantytown settlement, identifying him/herself as a certain ethnic group has very different implications than doing the same in their previous home area. This identification differs in terms of the name of the ethnic group, its structure, roles, the selection of leadership, and the overall influence of the ethnic unit in the life course of the individuals.

Furthermore, it is noticeable that though people identify themselves as being from one ethnic group in the shantytown, their overall social practices, attitudes and behaviors might differ considerably amongst them, to the extent that it is hard to recognize them as a collective single social entity. Having recognized this issue, I started to search for another way to categorize the people of Al-Baraka. Accordingly, I sought a kind of categorization that is able to include their actual life activities, perceptions, or their life practices: more precisely their own lifestyle. Clearly, in some dimensions it makes sense to refer to ethnicity, when describing people who employ it directly in their daily life activities; in other dimensions, namely when it comes to social structure, lifestyle[17] is more meaningful.

[17] The concept of 'milieu' seems also appropriate when comparing and contrasting between different lifestyles, as *"The concept of* "milieu" … is one approach to capture socio-economic and socio-cultural differences and promises a better understanding of the growing societal plurality of the global South" (Neubert 2013: 32).

3.2 The Concept of Lifestyle[18]

Lifestyle, according to the Cambridge Dictionary of Sociology 2006, "refers to relatively distinctive patterns of action and culture that differentiate people...[and the] expressive modes of behavior that forge collective patterns of living… [which] the study of lifestyle is employed to emphasize distinctions at the level of practice within wider frameworks of culture and power." Lifestyle as a concept has a more popular usage in sociology, following Pierre Bourdieu's usage of the concept in his seminal work *Distinctions* (1979 [trans. 1984]), where he argues that in modern class societies there are different groups within every class that have different activities and "tastes", which in turn gives the group a sense of solidarity (Turner 2006: 339).

Anthropologists and cultural studies scholars use the concept of subculture in a rather similar way to differentiate between different in-group segments of people, who are perceived as a deviation from a dominant culture: "the meaning of subculture is, then, always in dispute, and style is the area in which the opposing definitions clash with most dramatic force… the process whereby objects are made to mean and mean again as 'style' in subculture" (Hebdige 2002: 3). Mainly youth groups and negatively stereotyped minorities were studied using this concept. However, a more classical example of using subculture to study wide range of population in urban areas appeared in Oscar Lewis' seminal work Five Families (1959; Lewis 1988: 310), where he attempted to link poverty in urban areas to certain behavioral and social characteristics rather than simply economic deprivation markers: he later preferred to use the famous term "culture of poverty." A few decades later his concept was fiercely criticized for its alleged bias against poor people by blaming

[18] The definition of 'lifestyle group' in this study is based on two points: Firstly, the *Sage Dictionary of Sociology* defines "group" as individuals "defined by informal or formal criteria of membership, who have some shared sense of identity or are bound by relatively stable patterns of social interaction" (Sage 2006: 128); clearly lifestyle groups in Al-Baraka community fit all of these criteria, even if they are not recognized by their members as structured groups. Secondly, the *Cambridge Dictionary of Sociology* distinguishes between two theoretical bases for defining a group: (1) a group defined by outsiders, which has no social reality for its members (i.e. some sociological category, such as single-income families in rural areas); and (2) groups defined as such by their members through patterns of interaction and shared representations (Cambridge 2006: 255). Accordingly, I use the first type of definition for lifestyle groups in Al-Baraka.

them for their own poverty, and for portraying their situation as stagnant and naturally hereditary.

Another important anthropological contribution dealing with the concept of lifestyle in the Sudanese context is Beck's chapter entitled 'Tribesmen, Townsmen and the Struggle over a Proper Lifestyle in Northern Kordofan,' in which he tried to illustrate the process of assimilation and hegemony of the high culture claimed by Nile Valley ethnic groups in northern Sudan towards the nomadic people of Kordofan region. While 'lifestyle' here clearly refers to the specific way of life adopted by the middle class people from northern Sudan, "the lifestyle of the Nile Valley, hailed as spiritually and materially superior, is transported outwards, and traditional lifestyles are attacked as incompatible with Islamic civilization" (Beck 1988: 258). In this sense, lifestyle has been used as an empirical and conceptual tool to delineate cultural and identity transformations on a national level in Sudan, specifically describing how the dominant northern ethnic groups have been able to enforce their specific version of 'high culture' upon nomadic communities.

In my study, I have similarly tried to use lifestyle as an empirical and conceptual tool to manifest the specific materiality, activities and meanings attributed to different social groups and milieus in Al-Baraka. The conception of lifestyle used in my study is to describe the different ways of life that exist within one community of shantytown settlers, to enable this thesis to differentiate between various sets of behaviors and activities generated from different sources (i.e. rural home areas, middle class northerners, and global youth culture). This specific usage is more in line with sociologists' conception of lifestyle or milieu as a sub-group within a class system.

I argue that using lifestyle, as the main way of categorizing the people of Al-Baraka can offer many advantages. First, it enables categorizing people according to what they are actually doing in their course of daily life, thus avoiding the problem of relying predominantly on what is expressed verbally. This is based upon the idea that what people express verbally represents only some parts of their reality. Secondly, using lifestyle as a basis for categorization enables this research to be more flexible and comprehensive, including as many different components and attitudes as possible from the everyday life of the people in the shantytown. Besides the ethnic identification of the residents, other factors have strong influences on the life of particularly younger generations, such as issues like education, occupations, wealth, technology and gender.

Applying this new method of categorization is complex: defining lifestyle or the way of life is not an easy task given that identifying all different courses of life and accounting for all daily activities of shanty-towns settlers is virtually impossible. It would be misleading to imply that the proposed lifestyle categorization here would be exhaustive in encapsulating all the different ways of life currently existing in Al-Baraka. Here, I will try to apply a very broad categorization whereby all possible members and every possible way of life can be, in theory, included. This also might help us to understand and analyze the overall social structure in a more abstract way, in turn helping to make broader comparisons with other shantytown communities inside Khartoum or elsewhere.

After thorough examination of the data that I collected during the course of the two field trips to Al-Baraka, this thesis suggests that three broad categories of lifestyle groups can be assumed to exist in Al-Baraka shantytown, namely: the first generation, the educated people, and the second generation. Each could stand as a distinctive social lifestyle, in a sense that it has a specific structure and a unique lifestyle. More importantly, every lifestyle group has its own legitimacy and recognition by other lifestyle groups, regardless of whether that recognition takes the form of appreciation or condemnation.

3.3 The Concept of Social Practice

This concept is central and connected to the lifestyle concept; everyday life entails thousands of small elements of different social practices. While the exact definition of 'practice' is controversial among scholars and researchers, there is a general tendency to regard a wide array of "forms of bodily activities, forms of mental activities, 'things' and their use, a background knowledge in the form of understanding, know-how, states of emotion and motivational knowledge" (Shove et al. 2012: 7) as practices.

Theories of social practices focus on shared experiences, understanding, norms, meanings and practical knowledge, which are all considered part of the classical subjects of 'social phenomena.' More recently, the focus has shifted from taking social practice as the mere production of individual actors, to acknowledging and analyzing it as 'practice-as-entity,' whereby people are perceived as carriers of the practice through their performances. The key feature of this new approach is that "practices are constituted through the actions of material entities as well as people" (Shove et al. 2012: 9).

Furthermore, this approach maintains that social practice takes place in everyday life through interdependence of three elements: material, competence and meaning. Material refers to tools, infrastructure, objects, hardware, and even the body. Competence indicates practical knowledge, skills and appropriate performances. Meaning deals with the social and symbolic significance of things, mental activities and emotional or motivational knowledge. Through the combinations of these three elements, the specific practices evolve and change.

Applying the concept of social practice as outlined above on the case of Al-Baraka community seems very useful. Every lifestyle is constituted of specific arrangements of socially recognized practices, which comprise certain usages of materials, competences and meanings (as we will see in Chapters Four to Seven). In this sense, social practice plays a key role in defining what constitutes a lifestyle. Because the emphasis here in on social practice as a social entity and performance, a lifestyle can thus be perceived as an entity in constant evolution and re-construction through the practices of the actors.

3.4. The Concept of Ethnic Identity

Many scholars of urbanization in Africa have acknowledged the unique character of ethnic identity in African urban settlements, in comparison with ethnic identification in rural areas. The specific characters of ethnicity in urban settlements were particularly observed by early anthropologists who studied Copperbelt[19] towns in the 1950s. Mitchell analyzed the process of ethnic categorization much further, revealing how, despite the large number of ethnic groups represented on the Copperbelt, the whole of the African urban population was broken down and delimited within a very restricted number of broad ethnic categories. Knowledge about an alien ethnic group, its language, culture and system of social relations is determined by geographical and social distance. Ethnic groups that are territorially near one another will be very aware of hostilities and the cultural and historical distinctions that divide them. Such matters are beyond the knowledge of the outsider living outside that territory. Such a person's awareness of the distant ethnic groups is likely to be fragmentary, so that s/he would tend to ignore their internal differences and put them all altogether, treating them as a single ethnic entity (Epstein 1992).

[19] The account of the Manchester school of African urbanism is rather short here, as this thesis does not use their conceptions or methodology extensively.

Although ethnic identity was initially brought to cities from the countryside, its specific meaning and usage varies considerably. The first generation broadly assume that their usage of ethnic groups in the shantytowns is an expression of the continuation of the way of life in rural areas, as they try to promote the social organization of rural ethnic groups as the main structure of communities in the shantytown. Other elders consider it as a way of refusing urban life, and use ethnicity as a vehicle to keep themselves separate and distinct. However, many differences exist between ethnic groups in their original areas and in urban shantytowns; this is a result of the variations of environment and socio-economic organizations that prevails in urban areas.

In the case of Al-Baraka, if we try to account for the differences between ethnic group identities in rural areas and urban areas, there is first a difference in the structure of the ethnic groups. This takes the form of formal organization in the shantytowns, especially through ethnic associations, which need to be registered officially and organized according to a certain conventional bureaucratic hierarchy. By contrast, in the original community, traditional organization remains allied with the colonial and post-colonial governments. This organization also differs in the specific functions performed. In shantytowns, ethnic affiliations tend to fulfill the socio-cultural aspects of people's lives, connecting them mainly through popular gatherings for social occasions, considering that people are scattered in different locations. However, in home areas, ethnic groups still perform the functions of controlling the political and economic resources, through representing the communities politically and controlling lands.

Another significant difference is the way in which people select their ethnic leaders. In home areas, this tends to be in the hands of royal or hereditary kinship with historical roots; if there is any change in the balance of power among educated elites, this is usually undertaken internally within this elite kinship group. This happened recently in Darfur, where native administrations have undergone considerable changes over the last decades, owing to an apparent shift in people's perceptions. In order to cope with the increasing need for modernization and communication with the outside world and government officials in urban centers, many ethnic groups have promoted young, educated leaders to take posts in the system of native administration: for example, the Habbaniya and Birgid have selected retired generals as their paramount chiefs, and the Mima selected a university graduate as the deputy paramount chief (Abdul-Jalil 2007).

However, in Khartoum shantytowns, people have used very different methods to select their leaders. They were selected according to their experience in urban areas, as well as their abilities to deal with different individuals or groups involved inside or outside the shantytowns. This is because, in shantytowns, the everyday life of its local people no longer depends upon a community that shares the same history, blood origin and livelihood activities. This diversity allowed people to move towards making alternative strategic choices and using more urban methods. Today, in Al-Baraka, there is an Omda who belong to the royal family in Darfur, but he hardly has any influence in comparison to other ethnic leaders locally; some other local elders are more respected, because they did a lot of work in the community in the time before the planning of the area. Moreover, the local committees assume much more power and respect, whether inside Al-Baraka community or with other actors who are dealing with the community, such as government or NGOs.

3.5 The Practices of Ethnicity

The theoretical basis for ethnicity studies was long centered on two oppositional debates. Firstly, there was the long and heated controversy over primordialism and instrumentalism, namely whether ethnic identity was 'primordial,' profoundly rooted in and produced of collective cultural experiences, or if it arose as an *ad hoc* extension of political strategies.

A powerful defence of the instrumentalist approach was represented in Abner Cohen's work on urban ethnicity in Africa (1969, 1974), illustrating the consistent manipulation of kinship and cultural symbols by political entrepreneurs seeking political gains. This perspective remains popular in identity politics studies. The primordialist view is strongly represented in the works of Clifford Geertz, arguing along hermeneutic lines that socio-cultural systems are self-sustaining and were thus not subject to the wilful manipulation of individuals, in an approach that he engaged when writing about nationhood in the Third World. Usually, however, ethnicity studies in recent literature are viewed as instrumentalist in their basic orientation (Eriksen 1993).

The second debate, usually framed as the opposition between constructivism and essentialism, concerns the question of whether ethnic or national communities are created more or less consciously, or whether they grow organically, as it were, out of pre-existing cultural communities. In nationalism studies, the most extreme antagonist's position regarding the constructivism-essentialism issue is from the late Ernest

Gellner. While Anthony D. Smith developed a more moderate position in emphasizing the value of pre-existing ethnicities for the development of nationalism, while acknowledging its essentially modern character, Gellner pioneered the view that nations are totally modern creations—as an extension of industrialism and the modern state—which re-invent their past to achieve the appearance of antiquity and deep roots (Eriksen 1993).

The case of the Al-Baraka community suggests that the dynamics of ethnic groups' social life revolve on an instrumentalist-constructivist basis. The best way to prove this is to provide a brief account of how people construct their own reality, considering themselves as distinct ethnic groups. This also suggests that categorizing local people according to their ethnic groups would ease the difficulties of describing segments of population collectively. However, the dilemma remains concerning the extent to which this description can reflect the most significant differences between people; besides the ethnic differences recognized by people in their daily life practices, there are other more prominent social practices not based upon ethnic categorization.

All the people I interviewed in the course of fieldwork agreed that the Fur ethnic group[20] is the largest in the area, since Al-Baraka's establishment. However, some of them mentioned that, in reality, there are many ethnic groups that identify themselves as Fur in Al-Baraka or in the capital in general, yet consider themselves in Darfur as distinct ethnic groups to the Fur, even sometimes identifying themselves as the Fur's traditional rivals, like the Dagu and Berti. Their efforts to fall under the umbrella of Fur in Khartoum seem to be based upon their proximity in their original areas in Darfur and their many shared similarities in their way of life and culture. More importantly, they want to use their sheer number as a collective 'Fur' in Al-Baraka to have a greater share of power and resources in the area. Another factor is their realization that the role of ethnic group in the capital is very different to their home areas; this makes it nonsensical to adhere to old categorizations and old rivalries. Even their allegiance to the Fur ethnic group comes as a logical option, as the Fur had been a well-known empire ruling the region for several centuries in the past, and the whole home region was named after

[20] There are many similarities between Fur and Nuba ethnic groups in terms of how they organize their lives in Al-Baraka, although many socio-cultural variations exist in the original homelands. For this reason, I confine my descriptions to Fur and Southern ethnic groups.

them, suggesting that all other ethnic groups from different regions can more easily identify a person when he is from the Fur, compared to a "Gimer", for example.[21] The same phenomenon happened with people from the southern regions of Sudan, albeit with a different reference point, in using the geographical region (i.e. 'the south') to identify all ethnic groups as belonging to a regional unit.

Fur people dominated Quarter No. 2, but they are also the majority in Quarter No. 1, which led to locals dividing this quarter into two local committees, due to the dispute between Fur and Nuba and Southern people concerning who should be members in the local committees.

Among the Fur people, there were many ethnic associations, organized by areas and villages in Darfur, or sometimes by kinship groups, although they also cross-cut with neighborhood associations. This cross-cutting is very clear in the types of money contribution that a person can receive when he/she has a social occasion in his/her family: there is a list of his area of origin association, his father's linage, mother's linage, his neighbors and friends, and he/she uses the equipments of the neighborhood association to receive all those people in his/her house and neighbours' houses.

Fur people are famous for their adherence to tradition, especially to the Islamic religion and the Fur language. They are Muslim, and have a long tradition of Islamic schools (*khalwa*) where children are enrolled from an early age to learn the Quran and other Islamic principles. This means that most of the men and women know how to read and write Arabic and recite many verses of the Quran, as well as attending mosques to perform the five prayers. Although they also believe in Sufi Islam, usually they follow the *Tijaniyah* brotherhood. In North Sudan many people are also Muslims, and adhere to other Sufi sects, but in the cities modern Islam (i.e. urban Islam) is more prevalent and urban Muslims consider Sufi Islam as less 'original.' This urban Islam dominates urban areas in Sudan, especially in recent decades owing to the rise of the Islamic Brotherhood, which transformed urban Islam into the main root ideology for the government, propagated through media and educational policies. Because local children (the second generation) were born and raised in the Al-Baraka urban area, they believe more widely in the modern (urban) Islam, which has put them into dispute with the first generation in the mosques. This religious difference extends to many other aspects of life beyond religious philosophy; for example the belief in the mystical

---

[21] A comparably small ethnic group in Darfur, little known outside the original territory.

power of the Sufi leaders and their unlimited power, which can help people to achieve what they want through verses of the Quran or blessings from Sufi sheikhs. These differences in traditions are observed in many urban settings in Sudan. Earlier sociological models of religious studies tried to analyze these differences by differentiating between great and little Islamic traditions, or orthodox and popular Islam, or even between orthodox urban-based and mystical rural. These approaches are valuable descriptively, but clearly simplify the complexity of each tradition, as well as exaggerating the differences between them (Kenyon 2004: 24).

Another aspect of Fur life is their use of the Fur language, especially in the social gatherings where the majority has kinship relations. However, the Fur have less tendency to use their language when there are people from other ethnic groups present, or when the interaction is taking place in formal or modern situations. For the second generation, there are different attitudes towards using their indigenous languages; while many of them can understand it, because their parents and relatives usually use it, many of them cannot speak it fluently, and prefer to use Arabic even in their homes. Even for those who know Fur and can speak it, it is difficult for them to understand it fully, as it is only their second language. Another reason for some people's avoidance of the Fur language is the fact that it is considered as a less-urbanized behavior. It is seen as indicating that the person is a new rural arrival to the city. On the other hand, using proper urban Arabic is an indicator of being a 'fully urbanized' person. Under these pressures, even some of the first generation individuals prefer the use of proper Arabic, confining the use of the Fur language to very limited situations. This provides a clear example of the linguistic practices and competence in speaking and meaning of that practice, in which the meaning of a language a person might choose is linked directly to his/her competence in using that language.

In Al-Baraka we can also see Fur people practicing endogamous marriage between relatives, which is the preferable method for the majority of Fur ethnic groups, even in their original home areas. However, intermarriage with other ethnic groups out of the Fur umbrella does occur from time to time, particularly amongst the second generations, since basic education and living in the mixed quarters have enabled intermingling. One way to pursue interethnic marriage is through having a child before marriage, which forces the family to accept the man. Another contributing factor is the simple tradition of marriage in Fur cultures, and its low cost compared with other southern groups or with other groups in middle class areas. However, the acceptance of intermarriage from outside the Fur is usually very restricted for Muslims, and especially for their daughters; for this reason, many of the intermarriages with southern people take place between men from Fur and women from southern groups. My informants agreed that most intermarriage is practiced between different Fur sub-groups, or between Fur and Nuba, with fewer marriages with Baggara Arabs and southern people. These complex marriage practices indicate the many layers of meanings and competences presumed in the selections of a partner, and their acceptance from their respective families.

The second 'ethnic group' in the area in term of numbers is the southern people. This name is also an urban advent. Because 'southern people' as a nomenclature incorporates many different ethnic groups from different areas of the southern provinces, as 'southerners' have many different traditions, costumes, languages and beliefs, all originating from their particular place of origin in the southern regions of Sudan. Most people living in Al-Baraka from the south are Dinka, Shilluk, Nuer and what are called Equatorial tribes. The majority of people from these ethnic groups live in Quarters No. 2, 3, and the older inhabitants in No. 1.

The forced migration of the Southern people was on a larger scale than other ethnic groups, largely because there was no large-scale migration to the capital prior to the second civil wars in the South starting from 1983. The intensity of the war pushed millions of people to flee from their home areas, with many finding their way to the capital and then joining the small number who migrated before 1983 in the squatter settlements.

As previously noted, the differences in religion and language practices between the host community of Khartoum and the southern people put further distance between the two groups, and challenged processes of "assimilation," which supposedly should take place as soon as the migrants settle in an urban environment. However, many changes have been taking place especially between the second generation and the educated elites among the southern communities. This process has a long history, even in the southern region, as Francis Deng put it clearly in his account of Dinka people in the south in the 1970s. He stated that intergenerational conflicts in kinship and family were not always so consistent. In fact, the older members of society recognized their modernizing educated peers, and despite viewing them with respect due to their alien knowledge and practices through international education, the traditionalist elders included their newly educated fellow Dinka in decision-making processes. In turn, the 'modernized' educated members of society showed respect to the traditional chiefs, and their voice was supposedly channeled officially through these seniors. In other words, the structural relations usually remained on traditional lines. The traditional authorities saw in their modernizing relatives a source of upward social status for the kinship and family networks, and would form the basis for wider influence in intergroup arenas. However, the chiefs and their circles of subordinate chiefs increasingly viewed this remolding of family and kinship power processes as a danger to traditional values and ethnic institutions. This is heightened as the increasingly modern and educated youth see the position of the chief as undemocratic and exclusive. Educated youth in the 1970s viewed themselves as being commissioned as leaders by their descent groups, precisely because they believe that in the tribal arenas, and especially vis-à-vis the chiefs, they were able to see things that the traditional chiefs cannot see, and therefore are better able to protect their family rights. These modernizing sections of society were thus considered as a threat to the chiefs (Deng 1987).

It is clear now that the way of life that prevails in the shantytown of Al-Baraka, whether for the Fur or southern people, involves many urban aspects and significant changes as result of their migration. If we generate a theoretical interpretation for those changes by necessity, it might suggest that any kind of primordial or essentialist interpretation is misleading. Following Eriksen's general framework, "in anthropology at least, the recent shift towards the study of identities rather than cultures has entailed an intense focus on conscious agency and reflexivity; and for many anthropologists, essentialism and primordialism appear as dated as pre-Darwinian biology" (Eriksen 1993).

3.6 Social Structure of Al-Baraka

The prevailing assumption that can be found even in acclaimed slums studies and ethnicity studies is that all slum dwellers or urban poor are the same, and their communities have very little difference in their main features and characteristics, to the extent that all shantytown residents might be assumed to be one social group. An example from slum studies is Davis, who concludes by asserting a very general statement that "the root cause of urban slumming seems to lie not in urban poverty but in urban wealth" (Davis 2006: 95-96). Another example of undifferentiated categorization from ethnicity studies is Sondra Hale's study of Nubian communities in the Khartoum conurbation. "Through neighborhood clustering, occupational exclusiveness via nepotism and patronage, and voluntary associations, Nubians have articulated and maintained their identity in the public domain" (Hale 1979: 24-25). How-ever, many different social groups live in the complex shantytown communities, based upon different social and economic variables that contribute to the formation of the neighborhoods.

To understand Al-Baraka community we need to better know its social structure, or more precisely the internal classifications of its population. As I stated before, during my first days in the field I asked people about the way in which they defined themselves and other people, whereby all my informants agreed that they usually use their ethnic identification as a basis of classification, given that everybody know his/her ethnic group and many people are called after their tribal names. However, with more experience in the field I came to realize that while many people identify themselves as from one ethnic group, they actually perform different daily practices and hold different values and perceptions, and in fact members of the same ethnic group often have very little in common. For this reason, I started to use 'lifestyle' as the main concept to analyze and categorize the different social groups that co-exist in the Al-Baraka area. This also enabled me to differentiate between verbal identification, where people use ethnicity as the primary marker, and practiced identity, where it is possible to see other social markers through the performance and social practice of individuals and groups, as their lifestyles.

As we can see in this study, sometimes this lifestyle might differ from what people perceive and imagine about themselves, or how people identify themselves verbally. Verbal identity refers to how people perceive and define themselves orally, and does not necessarily accord with what they are practicing. Verbal identity can be obtained through asking people directly about their personal belonging, and how they engage with their identified community. In contrast, the way in which we can recognize and measure the lifestyle of certain individuals and group is through observing and examining the daily activities of people or their life practices. Thus it is important to distinguish between verbal identity and practiced identity; the latter refers to what people assume as good behavior and practices in their everyday lives, and usually this position comes from the convergence of all lifestyles that are practiced across certain social lifestyles, as we will see in the example of Al-Baraka.

In Al-Baraka, the first generation, the educated people, and the second generation can be considered as the basic social lifestyles, formed as a direct result of the specific variables that created the shantytown settlements. These social lifestyles are based upon the distinct ways of life that people pursue, and the lifestyle or the specific daily practices and perceptions of certain groups in the community.

The best way to illustrate the relations between the three ways of life is by using this triangular diagram (see Figure No. 5). Each could stand as distinctive lifestyle group, in a sense that it has a specific structure and a unique lifestyle. More importantly, each lifestyle has its own legitimacy and recognition from other groups, regardless of whether that takes the form of appreciation or condemnation. This appreciation is generally from people who are sharing the same lifestyle, or from those in the very center of the triangle (the mediators), or other people who are scattered in the triangle, in the sense that they share more than one lifestyle. By contrast, those positioned in the corners receive condemnation from people in other corners; for example, ethnic and religious leaders' attitudes towards youth gangs. I went to many social occasions and religious gatherings in the neighborhoods (e.g. funerals, Friday prayers), and every time I heard very harsh criticisms of gang members. I also heard the same criticisms (with different logics) from local committee members and teachers against 'gangsters' and school drop-out youths.

The 'first generation lifestyle' refers to people who aspire to be like their ancestors, organizing their life around fellow residents who have the same origins and beliefs, or their fellow tribesmen. They commonly talk about the glory of the past and their homeland, and how urban values are corrupting their people. Furthermore, they are engaged in serious efforts to maintain and disseminate their traditional values and practices. This is a large population in Al-Baraka, comprised especially of old people and first generation settlers who spent large parts of their adult lives in their home areas. They prefer to use native languages and dialects whenever possible, through interacting with their relatives or fellow tribesmen, usually in the public domains of regular social occasions such as birth naming ceremonies, marriage ceremonies and funerals. Through maintaining these social practices, first generation people consolidate their commitment to their traditions, as well as pushing other lifestyle groups to assert their obedience to the 'homeland' – and, by extension, to the first generation as elders. All families and relatives are obliged to attend these social occasions, particularly close relatives and kinsmen. It is an idealized social arena where people who do not respect traditions can be corrected, and if necessary punished, not least through public criticism.

The first generation residents endeavor to keep relations with their home area intact whenever possible, by maintaining communication with their relatives at home by different means, largely through visiting them, and hosting them when they visit the capital. They also engage in creating ethnic group organizations and regional associations based upon neighborhoods. Every small ethnic group, village or town in the home area has a kind of centralized association within each neighborhood; its main purpose is to gather the people of the homeland together and consolidate their social solidarity, although in many cases the activities are set up to serve the needs of the people in the shantytown, rather than critical issues of the home areas.

The 'educated people lifestyle' refers to a wide range of people, a mix of the first and second generation of residents. What they all share is some kind of formal education, which has allowed them to get better jobs and more economic and social resources. Generally, they are inspired by other parts of the city, and they try to copy and reproduce the urban middle class way of life. This not only includes accessing urban services, education or modern luxury goods, but also the use of cultural components of the urban northern middle class, such as the use of urban Arabic or English, and an emphasis on urban Islam or Christianity. Many people are adopting this way of life, and share the belief that the traditional way of life is backward.

The distinguishing feature of this lifestyle group comes from the high value placed on formal education, derived from the experiences of the first generation with local governments and other parts of the city. Since the arrival of the shantytown settlers to the city, all of their urban experiences have been heavily influenced by their hostile relations with the formal urban institutions (local government), which considered them as outsiders and a pathological threat to the capital. Educated people see their power and influence stemming from connections to specific institutions, whose physical presence in shantytowns provides essential instruments for the educated residents. Places like local committee houses, schools and development centers are at the heart of the power machine used by local educated people to achieve their leadership aspirations in the local community.

The younger 'second generation' has constructed their own distinct lifestyle, given that generally they have no strong affinity with their homeland or other parts of the city. They reach beyond the border and their immediate social reality by using modern technology and communication. In doing so they have been able to construct a strong connection with a global youth culture, usually expressed via global media. Through rap and reggae, Congolese music, American and Indian movies, American wrestling and satellite TV, they have re-invented themselves locally, in the form of local music cultures and a rap-influenced style of dressing and behavior. This second generation lifestyle has developed in certain spaces that are created and used exclusively by youth. These young residents meet in places such the stations, shisha cafés and music parties, and these are sites of interaction and mutual education in establishing a distinctive lifestyle, recognizing their power and agency, as well as being ready to make a difference. These spaces are vital to understanding and analyzing the second generation's construction of their separate lifestyle, and are a demonstration of the vibrant and dynamic processes of being part of the whole shantytown while maintaining a distinctive way of life.

In each corner of the theoretical triangle is one of these three lifestyles. People are thus scattered inside the triangle, some of whom are more 'attached' to one corner (e.g. gangs, teachers, tribal leaders), meaning that they confine their social relations and daily activities within their own small group, and have less tendency to interact with people who prioritize other lifestyles. The majority of the population is positioned between more than one extreme corner, given that they believe in some elements of more than one way of life. There are also others who are in the middle of the triangle, embracing elements of all the three lifestyles; these people are generally considered popular, and are friendly with all groups. Indeed, it seems that they represent the ideal position (i.e. as mediators).

For most of the population, opting for only one lifestyle is not ideal; people tend to combine two or three lifestyles at the same time. This is what makes the Al-Baraka residents distinct from their urban neighbors, and similarly distinct from their home area ancestors and relatives. Moreover, this is what gives shantytowns a unique overall identity that represents what people actually perceive as moral and ideal daily life practices. At the same time, people also acknowledge the fact that not everybody is able to meet the high standards of existing at the center of these lifestyles (as a mediator). This recognition gives people the freedom to choose what they think is appropriate for them. There is personal agency insofar as there are choices between lifestyle practices, although this is also conditioned by the competence of the individuals; in fact, the competence in acquiring the right practiced ability to function within a particular lifestyle and social culture is the most significant criteria for those assuming the position of a mediator.

For example, one of my close friends on my first field trip, a young man called Adam in his mid-twenties, worked as a shopkeeper in the neighborhood. He graduated from a trade school as a electrical technician, and subsequently worked for few years in a factory, before opening his shop. In front of his shop, young people gather daily in what they called the station, and they usually chat with Adam. Adam does not agree with the local youth about everything, and sometimes he criticizes their behaviors, especially in terms of traditions, religions, or even educational practices. Because he is maintaining a personal respect towards many aspects of Al-Baraka life, he speaks the Fur language, although he has only been to Darfur once. He goes to the mosque five times a day to pray, and follows all social occasions of his neighbors and relatives; however, he once told me that he does not believe in the ability of traditional religious methods of healing (e.g. amulets). Adam also maintains good relationships with the educated people in the neighborhood, who treat him as one of them. In this way, Adam is trustworthy to all people in the neighborhood, which might be one reason for his success in the retail business. After a short while, he was able to marry the daughter of his aunt. He continued to live with his parents, where he was able to construct a small room for himself.

People know that reaching the position of being a mediator is very difficult, yet an ideal 'rather imagined', and to ease these contradictions between the ideal practices 'very center' and the real everyday life 'lifestyles practices', people use instead their verbal identity 'ethnic identification'. This is possibly due to the nature of verbalized identity, which is inherited through birth and family, without the ability to control or change it, and carries significant cultural and 'traditional' weight. When people use their ethnic identification, they are often actually trying to acknowledge the difficulty in meeting the high standard of the ideal position of 'being a mediator,' or avoiding acknowledging their failure of doing so.

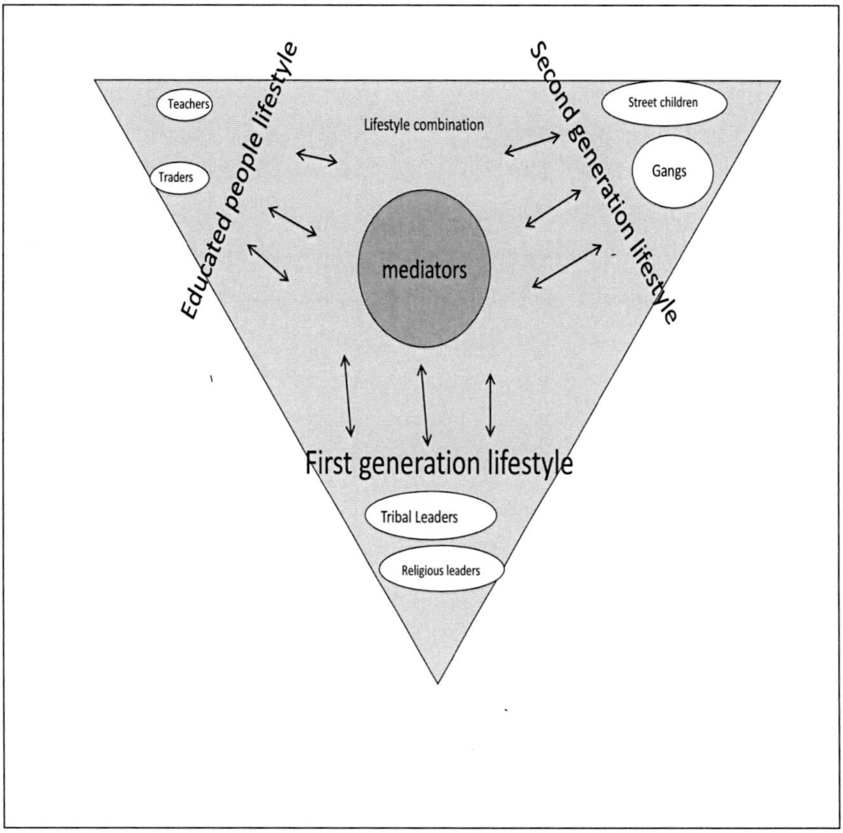

Figure 5: Diagram of Lifestyles in Al-Baraka

Chapter Four: The First Generation: Myth of Traditions

4.1 Introduction

In this chapter, I will concentrate on the first generations of residents, exploring how they have been able to construct their own specific lifestyle and use different social practices to generate different communal meanings, accompanied by different materiality and competences. The chapter will begin with an illustrative story from Al-Baraka, to give a sense of the relations and position of the first generation concerning daily life, as well as how they practice their authority and impose their specific meanings and materiality on everyday urban life. Subsequently, I will look at the composition of the first generation, the inner structure of the lifestyle group, and their relations with other lifestyle groups in Al-Baraka. Finally, I will conclude the chapter by examining the economic migrants and the forced migrants as two distinct sub-categories largely making up the first generation lifestyle group.

4.2 Slaughtering an Ox at Eid

To better understand Fur traditions, it was important to look at the events that take place in the neighborhood, to systematically clarify the relations between the first generation and other lifestyles. During my fieldwork, I participated in one regular event that takes place every year after the Ramadan holy month, when Fur people fast during the day and, after sunset, gather in the streets to break the fast together, praying then chatting for some time. There are three days of celebration after Ramadan, called (Eid Ramadan). It is a public holy day, since it is considered an Islamic celebration. Fur people augment to this celebration by slaughtering an ox and dividing the meat between neighbors; usually each group that breaks the fast together organizes this slaughtering. This account follows the course of this event.

Our neighborhood group breaking the fast in Ramadan was comprised of about twelve heads of families with their sons, as well as some bachelors like me. Since the beginning of Ramadan, there had been a discussion between the elders about the organization of the ox slaughtering at the end of the month. It appeared to be a specific organization that people had been doing every year. Firstly, the elders appointed Suliman to collect the money; he is a policeman in his mid-thirties, married with two children, and is well known in the neighborhood as a reliable person.

Soon, he announced the beginning of the collection of the money for the event, which was 1.5 SDG per day or 45 SDG for the whole month, whereby some individuals paid on a weekly basis and other just announced their interest and promised to pay in full at the end of the month. Suliman kept records of all these details. When the end of the month approached, the issue of slaughtering the ox became more frequent in conversations among the group, and many people registered names of their relatives who wanted to participate, who, despite not living in the neighborhood, communicated this through their relatives in the group.

On the morning of the second day of Eid, Suliman was outside his home with other three elder people, collecting the money from the participants. There were two registered people who could not pay their share, then two substituted them; others could not pay the full amount of money, Suliman called them to solve the problem, and ultimately 1160 SDG was collected. Suliman asked me to keep the money for them. We took a rickshaw to the animal market, and while we passed through the neighborhoods in Al-Baraka many groups started to slaughter their ox. Subsequently, we passed through a second-class neighborhood before reaching the market, where I noticed many empty plots with electricity already wired in, which is very rare. Someone told me that it is a new way for the government to attract buyers. When we reached the animal market, we started to look around, and one of the elders asked about a good ox, with the owner telling him the price was 1800 SDG. We chatted with another group who had also come to buy. Then a Fur person told both groups that there was a nearby farm where the prices were cheaper. We took his pick-up truck to that farm, which was very large and for cows and bulls, where we also found other groups. The elders chose an ox, for which the owner charged 1400 SDG, before a Fur mediator intervened. It seemed as if he had the trust of the owner and the purchasers alike, because he was known to the driver of the pick-up truck, who was known to the group, and he talked with them in the Fur language. After long negotiations, the two parties agreed upon 1200 SDG. One of the group members had money to add, and there were other expenses involved, like the three men who tied the ox and loaded it onto the pick-up truck, who subsequently asked for 45 SDG, as well as 6 SDG for the rope. However, after another brief negotiation, they agreed to 15 SDG for lifting the ox and 4 SDG for the rope.

We returned back to the house of Suliman, where we managed to put the ox down on the ground still roped, with a lot of joy from the children.

Before our journey, many people had come out to participate in the slaughtering process, although when we came back we could not find anyone. Suliman went to the nearby shop, where people usually gathered, and asked about them, whereupon he was told that they had gone to have their breakfast. Suliman complained that some people escape the hard work of slaughtering, and just come at the end to take their share of the meat. After half an hour, people started to come back reluctantly, then the process of slaughtering started, although we were only about eight people (see Figure No. 6). The head was cut by an older man, who had extensive experience, while others held the ox down during that painful operation. The problem was that all the knives were not sharp enough to cut the throat of the ox quickly, so it took much time and energy for all of us. As we started to remove the skin, more people joined us, while some went to call other people to come. Others dug a large hole in the ground in the street to fill it with the discarded parts of the ox. After removing the whole skin and unwanted parts, we moved inside the house of Suliman.

Suliman's house comprised one room build of green bricks (mud bricks), in front of which was a large verandah made of straw and wood. There were two beds and a mat on the ground, as well as a similar arrangement and an unfinished room on the other side of the house. I subsequently came to learn that the house is divided into three parts, with the other parts belonging to other brothers of Suliman.

People divided themselves into small groups, some taking responsibility for cutting the bones into small parts, some cutting the flesh, and some elders cleaned the intestine parts and cut them into small pieces. One of the elders took the head of the ox, while younger people focused on preparing food, sending a boy to bring coal, onions and spices from the nearby shop. They gave younger people the best parts of the meat and small parts of the liver and heart, with another youngster—a rickshaw driver—taking responsibility for preparing the tea.

The most important group, including Suliman and other elders, was responsible for dividing the meat, having brought a scale to weigh the meat out equally. The total number of participants reached 29, after adding one more participant to meet the extra expenses of the transportation and the preparation of the food and tea.

The language of conversation between the older people was Fur, apart from when a person spoke with someone who did not know the Fur language, or when they talked about something modern which had no equivalent in the Fur language. Meanwhile, the younger generation only used Arabic, as many cannot speak Fur fluently. This event compares with the experience of chatting during breaking fast in Ramadan, when most of the conversation took place in Arabic, with Fur only used when an elder man came and started talking in Fur. Thus, it seems that the slaughtering tends to be seen as a 'traditional' event, while having breakfast outside in the streets during Ramadan tends to be more urbanized, which dictates the usage of language.

When the butchery reached its final stages, in the afternoon at about four o'clock, the number of people grew to about thirty men, who divided into small groups to eat the food and drink the tea. While the food was not cooked particularly well because the amount of coal was insufficient to cook the meat properly, the young workers also took the best parts during its preparation; moreover, the number of people was far more than the intended numbers. Accordingly, the people who had worked very hard since morning were unhappy about the food. However, this did not seem to be a very important issue, as everyone was very happy with their share of the meat, each taking more than five kilos of different kinds of meat for only 45 SDG, which is around half the normal price in the market. Many of them appeared delighted about having this amount of meat, and especially the parts that can be dried *sharmût* and used later on, since dried meat is considered one of the important components of food for the Fur people.

The final part of the day was when Suliman started calling everyone from his list to take his portion (see Figure No. 7), whereby every part of the ox was divided equally between participants. Only the four legs, parts of intestine and part of the head were taken by some people who had participated from the beginning without having a share.

It is clear from this event that while the elders took responsibility for organizing more traditional events, they also relied on younger, more educated people, and to a lesser extent on the second generation. However, this inclusion is not open for everyone; rather, there are many criteria for choosing assistants from the educated or second generation. When the elders chose Suliman to keep the money and lead all the processes of the event, this choice was rational on many levels. Firstly, he could efficiently undertake all the tasks and responsibilities, owing to his experience as a policeman, giving him power within the community, as well as the ability to deal with people outside Al-Baraka in the animal market. Secondly, he is a respected person by all social groups, and particularly respected by the elders. He adheres to traditions, so by picking him the elders could encourage other members of the educated group and the second generation to be more like him.

This event takes place on a neighborhood basis, as the initiative and the organization of the event is executed by the members breaking the fast in the street. This includes people belonging to different ethnic groups under the umbrella of the Fur group, as well as others belonging to the Nuba ethnic group. However, in practice, many other people came and joined the group from outside the neighborhood, mainly comprising relatives of people in the group. Thus, when the event took place, it became more ethnically homogenous, which why the majority used the Fur language, and perhaps also because Fur people brought the tradition from their original area and are more experienced in slaughtering cows and oxen. In the end, the ox slaughtering event took the shape of a specifically ethnic event, despite having started as a heterogeneous neighborhood social event.

Figure 6: Photo of Slaughtering an Ox 1
The group starting the slaughter, Al-Baraka, 2010.

Figure 7: Photo of Slaughtering an Ox 2
At the end of the event, Suliman called on the participants to take their share of the meat. Al-Baraka, 2010.

4.3 First Generation Composition

The first generation of residents, *nâs kubâr*, refers to those who migrated firstly to Al-Baraka. More broadly it also refers to the people who spent most of their adult lives in their place of origin. Accordingly, they are well acquainted with the traditional way of life from their home areas.

It is necessary to bear in mind that there are many variations between individuals in this lifestyle, in terms of their individual abilities to adhere to the values and behaviors from the original area. There are also differences in their individual competence in adapting their behaviors to be more in accordance with the type of life that prevails in the shantytowns and urban setting generally. There may be many factors that determine the extent to which an individual is able to change in this sense, and to what extent s/he can preserve an older way of life from a home area. These factors can include:

—Educational level: an educational certificate is essential in finding a high ranking or paying job, which determines the extent and way in which an individual can develop strong ties with other parts of the city, or gain high status in Al-Baraka. For example, the people who represented the area at the time before re-planning were all tribal leaders, some of whom were illiterate; more educated people gradually started to replace them.

—The length of time spent in the town: the longer an individual stayed in Al-Baraka, the more s/he assumes the persona of an urban person, encouraged to try to imitate the behaviors and way of life imported from other parts of the city. Furthermore, the longer a person has stayed, the more s/he becomes familiar with the environment, particularly through encounters with different situations and interactions with different people from within or outside the area.

—The type and time of migration: some people and families migrated for economic reasons, others for security reasons, or to escape natural disasters. The first milieu has usually adapted to the city; they have better jobs, and their houses are usually built with concrete materials, contrasting with the second milieu. Older migrants (generally arriving in Khartoum for economic reasons) secured better places to live and are better off financially, as well as usually being well established socially. By contrast, forced migrants usually fled their home areas suddenly, migrated as groups without any resources, and thus lack any pre-knowledge about urban settlements. Although many IDPs choose to settle in rural areas, where they can find work in agriculture, the majority chose to settle in large cities, hoping to find assistance from NGOs and settling near their relatives in squatter settlements, and finding work in the informal sector.

—Cultural variations: the more people and individuals have cultural components that are similar to the urban sitting, the faster and easier they can adapt, including speaking the Arabic language and being Muslim. This can effectively influence the way in which a person interacts with those from other parts of the city. It is noticeable in Al-Baraka that while older settlers from the Fur and Nuba ethnic groups are more adapted to urban life, already being Muslim and speaking Arabic plays an important role in that adaptation, although these changes do not necessarily mean that they are fully Arabized or Islamized. Indeed, the question of Arab identity is so ambiguous to the point where it almost defies concrete analysis. The ability to speak Arabic does not necessarily mean one is Arab; for instance, the Berti and Birgid have lost their vernacular languages within the last century or so, but seemingly do not yet regard themselves as Arab (O'Fahey 2008: 12). They may or may not do that, or be able to do that, in the future. More precisely, in Sudan, Arabs are those who claimed themselves as Arab, and have fictional genealogies to prove it. The whole question is now politicized and used as a means to exclude or include some ethnicities. Moreover, for southern migrants, their adherence to Christianity and using traditional languages and English creates distance between them and other ethnic groups.

—Racial discrimination: according to the ethnic hierarchy that prevails in the northern parts of Sudan, people from southern Sudan are considered as having the lowest status, stereotyped as being descendants of slaves, with this position consolidated by other urban factors (e.g. illiteracy and poverty). In comparison, people from so-called western Sudan (e.g. the Fur, Nuba) are considered better than southern people, albeit just because they are Muslims and speak Arabic, although ultimately they are also towards the bottom of the hierarchy. This discriminatory factor works as a counter to the ability of shantytown dwellers integrating and assimilating into city culture; thus, whenever a shantytown resident crosses Al-Baraka boundaries to other parts of the city, there are extremely obvious behaviors and values that reminds them of their exact position in the city social ladder, which is likely to persuade them to be more adherent to their original traditions.

There are many similarities between different individuals of the first generation of settlers, the majority of whom adhere to their familial traditions, and most of whom believe that the ideal life is one belonging to the home area. As such, the more a person performs and replicates the traditions of original home life, the more s/he becomes a good person. While this might be a largely romantic view, nevertheless the way of life and the kind of activities those people pursue can give us a clear understanding of the extent to which these residents genuinely believe in their glorious past. Other studies suggest that the same pattern exists in similar situations, such as the expressions of conservative Red Xhosa in the African township of East London.

> "This conservative ideal, which has been noticed as typical of the Red Xhosa, in country and town alike, works in two ways. First there is the negative aspect: Red people are hostile on principal to most non-Red institutions, and therefore avoid most of the available associations, churches, amusements, and urban-style amenities, and also such innovations as having married women come to earn money in towns… Secondly there is the positive aspect. A 'good' Red man must remain committed to Red institutions or habits for the very reason that they are Red. He must value the ways of the

> ancestors, 'who like people to go on living in the way they themselves used to live'. Conservatism, i.e. continuance in specifically Red ways, is equated with tribal loyalty" (Mayer 1971: 285).

Initially, these older residents preferred using vernacular languages and dialects, whenever possible, and understandably that is not possible unless the person interacts with his kinfolks or fellow tribesman. The most effective means of doing this was by preserving regular social occasions such as birth naming ceremonies, marriage and funerals. Through maintaining these social occasions, people consolidate their commitment to traditions, as well as declaring their obedience to the first generation, as all families and relatives are obliged to attend them depending on their degree of kinship relation. This is also the arena in which people who do not respect tradition can be corrected, and if necessary punished.

Keeping relations with the original area intact whenever possible can only be achieved by maintaining communication with relatives all the time through different means: by visiting them, treating them well when they come to the capital for various reasons, especially for using urban services (health, education, etc.), as well as maintaining a regular exchange of information between the shantytown in the capital and the home area. Technology has considerably helped in maintaining regular contact with home via mobile phones.

In the same way, by creating ethnic and regional associations, each ethnic group or home village/town within a different neighborhood has a kind of centralized organization; this mostly tries to adopt the same administrative structure as in the original area. This perhaps only differs in the case of ethnic groups who have no central political structure (a segmentary system) in their original areas, like the Dinka and Nuer; in their cases, the centralized structure comes as a way of adapting to urban life, following other ethnic groups. Leadership is not usually from the same royal families of the original area, which opens the door to other criteria of leadership selection, influenced by town circumstances, like the importance placed on being a long-term resident, and having contacts with other ethnic groups in the area. As Ahmed, one of the tribal leaders from the Nuba people (Lafofa), stated:

> "the way that a person can be chosen is depending on his morality and ability to solve the problems, because the responsibility is just wisdom from

> the God…when people know that someone able to solve the problems between people, then will take him and put him as a chief."[22]

The result of all these efforts by the first generation to maintain the traditions of their original areas is that the majority of the population—even from other lifestyles such as educated people and the second generation—respect older traditions, at least publicly. The role played by women, and especially older women, is very important here in terms of keeping traditions. They are the mothers, aunts and grandmothers who place significant pressure on the community to maintain standards, even upon elder men.

Women usually communicate less with people outside the shantytown; indeed, even when women work, the majority do so on an informal basis, in agriculture or domestic services in neighboring middle class areas. Their social network is mostly confined to their relatives and neighbors, and these are the main source of social pressure. Ultimately, it appeared that women adhere more to older traditions, and men are enforced to observe the traditions. It is possible to assume that women's approval of new 'traditions', while not being entirely a matter of a free choice, is more likely to be a sign of deeper ambiguities in the social practices of shantytowns. Who a woman comes into contact with, and how these social relationships affect her, plays an important role in the personal changes she chooses—or declines—to take. In that regard, the views of former displaced Sudanese women in Khartoum are wide-ranging and diverse (Abusharaf 2009: 14). However, it is easy for men to use their greater social power to change the course of events based upon their own interests. Moreover, if necessary, they can use the extra-power from the same traditions to force other members of their families or community to adhere to what they want. In practice, 'tradition' is not an absolute act that people follow whatever the cost; rather, it is a rational choice that the first generation men and women use to gain benefits. Even the use of traditions as an ideology and way of life is ultimately also a rational choice, in the sense that, for first generation residents, pursuing this way of life gives them social power and self-assurance among other lifestyle groups in the area, as well as a vehicle for resistance to the more affluent other parts of the city.

---

[22] Interview with Ahmed, an ethnic leader from Nuba Mountains, Al-Baraka, 17 July 2010.

Furthermore, the first generation generally tries to practice the form of religion, especially Sufi Islam, which exists in their original area in so-called western Sudan (Fur, Nuba people). While the principles of Islam are heavily advocated in Al-Baraka based upon the influences of the mass media and other parts of the city, it is obvious that this kind of advocated Islam is different to local practices (i.e. urban Islam). The two sub-systems of belief coexist, with more emphasis on 'traditional' Sufi Islam from the first generation and from religious leaders (Imams) of the many mosques that spread in all quarters, and especially Quarters 1 and 2, where many Fur people live. This has led to some tensions among young educated people, who grew up in the capital and are more accustomed to urban Islam, having learnt it through formal education, the media, and regular contact with other parts of the city. On many occasions, I heard young people accuse the Imam of the nearby mosque—and the people who control its affairs—of being 'backwards', believing in things that do not belong to true Islam. The Imam criticized the young generation several times through his Friday sermon, directly mentioning youth behaviors and the excessive use of technology. He specifically used the example of the youth gangs called *negarz*, and encouraged their fathers and the first generation residents to take responsibility to teach good behavior to their children from an early age. While it seems as if he was unable to counter the criticism of the young educated people, he consistently tried to remind the prayers about Sufi principles mixed with many aspects of urban Islam. In an interview with Sheikh Suliman, who runs a *khalwa* in Quarter No. 4, he complained about this, saying: "The prophet said: the paradise is surrounded by difficulties, while the hell is surrounded by the enjoyments [sic], this why now the Negraz [sic] in the area now they have identity and completed organizational system, they have their own chief and secretary and financial secretary, and a lot of young people from the area joined them although they just started before two or three years, while we are working in teaching the Quran for 10 years, and we have less numbers than them [sic]."[23] This is an apparent example of the materiality related to different religious interpretations, which can be attributed to the different meaning that each lifestyle group assigns to its social practices.

The same relationships also exist within families; while women in areas of origin traditionally have freedom and ownership rights in western Sudan (among the Fur), more than that the conditions of poverty and

[23] Interview, Al Baraka, 30 September 2010.

the need for cash in Khartoum, many women have their own jobs, which in effect gives them even more freedom. This amount of freedom for women does not exist in other parts of the city, where more restrictive traditions exist. The most noticeable example is in relationships between men and women; for instance, while it is not easy to have sexual relations before marriage in middle class areas and it is considered an insult to family honor, in the shantytown it is not unusual to know that a girl has had a child before marriage. In fact, it is considered an effective way to pursue the man, or for her family to proceed in marriage ceremonies. This practice is very common in different ethnic groups, whether involving Fur, southern or Nuba people; indeed, it is only generally condemned by educated people.

When the first generation residents, or even educated people, describe the community, they usually referring to themselves by their respective ethnic group, although in reality there are no significant differences between these categories. Differences are not substantial and fundamental, and can be attributed to the different environments that people came from. Most importantly, all of them have some differences from the dominant culture in the city. Furthermore, people have shared many difficulties since their arrival in Al-Baraka, and these challenges have created a common history among them. For instance, residents initially mutually suffered from a lack of legal land ownership, water, electricity, transportation and good jobs, as well as being stereotyped as poor and IDPs by all other residents of the city.

Usually, the first generation residents use social gatherings to practice their authority and influence, especially in funerals, whether in mosques in the case of some Fur people (Karama) or in the neighborhood near the deceased's house, as in the case of Southern people. During one funeral that I attended in a Fur-dominated neighborhood, many elders spoke to the gathering inside the mosque after the midday prayer. All the speakers were religious people (Sheikhs) or ethnic leaders, most of whom talked about life and death from religious perspectives, reminding people about what is life after death. However, I noticed that all of them—after a while—switched to talking about their migration to Khartoum, with all speakers having come to the city before the 1970s, meaning that they have long urban experience. Subsequently, they talked about issues concerning the life of their local people, especially the *negarz* gangs, as well as their achievements in the past in solving the problems of the community.

In the case of southern people's funeral events, speeches initially focused on the deceased, including their life and achievements, before turning to other public issues. Educated young people and religious elders usually dominate the speeches, with dominant issues at the time being the referendum and independence from the north. These issues took precedence over local problems. Women followed these speeches with traditional and Bible verse songs.

4.4 Economic Migrants

At first glance, it is not easy to distinguish between economic migrants and those forced to move to Khartoum due to security issues or natural disasters. Distinguishing between populations requires a careful examination of the first generation group's disparate lives. What makes this particularly difficult is that the planning of Al-Baraka area was executed in a late stage in its development, after the area was highly settled; the government then came and gave every "eligible" family (in their definition) ownership of its house plot, all at the same size and price. This gave the area a sort of sameness, which makes it difficult to distinguish between the physical layouts of the neighborhood's houses.

Economic migrants largely made the journey to Khartoum as individuals, sometimes just for discovering a new life in the capital, where they generally succeeded in finding jobs, usually as unskilled workers in the industrial area in Khartoum North (Kober). At the beginning of their settlement in Khartoum, the migrant usually maintained strong relationships and personal commitment to his homeland, visiting his family every year, sending a share of his remittances regularly, and also potentially travelling to participate in agriculture in rainy season. When he accumulated enough money, he might return home and marry, then travel back with his wife to live together in Karton Shambat, adjacent to the industrial area in Kober. Many families typically stayed there until the early 1970s, when, under pressure from the local population of Shambat and government fears of the increasing numbers of squatters and the growth of the area, Karton Shambat was demolished and re-planned as a Fourth Class settlement in Wehda el Wataniya near Haj Yousif village. However, not all residents of Karton Shambat managed to find a plot in the new planned area; they thus created a new squatter settlement nearby, called Karton Kassala. Subsequently, many people displaced from different areas of Khartoum North found their way to Karton Kassala.

Many differences still remain among people based upon the time of their migration and the reasons behind it. For economic migrants who made the journey to the capital earlier, it was for economic reasons or as an adventure. Expecting to find better jobs and higher incomes, or to explore a new way of life, were broad reasons for migration between 1960 to 1980, coinciding with a boom in industrial activities in Khartoum North.

This early migration and work in the capital enabled these migrants to gradually adapt to the new environment, even with uncertainty surrounding their settlements, with frequent demolitions and moving houses. These residents also generally managed to forge stable careers, especially in government institutions, although the decline of industrial activity in the 1990s halted the careers of many, forcing them to join the thriving informal sector. These workers managed to do relatively well compared to their recent counterparts, benefiting from their accumulated competence and skills in the city; for instance, they had the necessary language skills (i.e. urban northern Sudan dialects of Arabic), which is essential for trading well in the informal market, as well as knowing where opportunities were located and maintaining a crucial a social network for business.

The economic composition of the majority of the first generation migrants includes workers in government institutions, lower ranks in the armed forces, workers in small factories as unskilled laborers, construction workers and small traders. The first two sectors are mostly dominated by older migrants, while migrants who could read and write, or learnt to do so through their work, could manage to climb the ladder and gain higher positions, especially in the national army, where promotion is more frequent and dependent upon years of work experience.

Such promotions, accumulated skills, and work networks boosted the status of economic migrants locally, giving them the ability to form a local leadership. However, such leadership is still acquired according to ethnic group. Every ethnic group continued to have its own chief, encouraged by the way in which people were living at that time, where each ethnic group formed a neighborhood enclave. Within these neighborhoods, people chose their leadership largely upon their experience and skills, especially experience in solving problems between people, and particularly among neighbors. When people became aware of a person's competence in terms of solving disputes, then people typically opted to select this person to represent them.

This helped economic migrants to represent their ethnic groups against others. This could be considered as the first break away from the traditional tribal system, where leadership is exclusively for the royal kinship. While in some ethnic groups, the Khartoum leader needed to be approved by the central leadership in their original area, this was mostly a matter of symbolic recognition, as long as the lives of local people received very little contact and influence from their leaders in the homeland. This further opened the door for new methods of selecting local ethnic leaders in Khartoum, where people could participate directly through elections or by approving the chiefs, sometimes also with the involvement of outside powers like the government or political parties. Accordingly, urban ways of organizing and meanings of power structures found their way into the shantytowns' political life.

In this way, economic or early migrants could accumulate higher social status, combined with a better economic position and more material gains, in line with their original ultimate goal of being in the capital to improve their economic profile. For some, this goal freed them more from obligation towards their home areas: they already had ideas and intentions about life in Khartoum, and planned to stay perhaps for their whole life. This supported economic migrants in making financial gains, living in more strategic locations, and owning more valuable houses; their building materials were also more durable, and their children could afford to enroll in the few schools available at that time.

These residents became a hub for their relatives from their home areas, who were increasingly obliged to find their way to the capital to seek social services, or to live permanently, trying to imitate their successful host relatives in the shantytowns. While, for the casual observer, shantytowns seem like the periphery of the city, or its least urbanized parts, in fact they are an urban center for huge numbers of relatives regularly visiting from rural areas.

The trajectory of activities for the economic migrants seems more diverse and mobile than their forced migrant counterparts. This is partly based on their social network, which started with neighbors whom they have known for more than twenty years, before and after the planning of the area. With these long-term contacts, their mutual historical challenges, and their children growing up together, neighborhood relations were likely stronger than ethnic relations. People still communicate and socialize with their relatives and their ethnic groups, some of whom are also neighbors, and maintain relationships with their original areas through visitors or through travel to their homeland, especially for social occasions. Thus the dominant aspect of their social network is their relationship with other nearby shantytowns, particularly within their core area (i.e. the old planned shantytown) where people usually go to the market to buy food or other goods, as well as going there for entertainment and to meet their close friends. Another important arena for communicating with others is through working outside the core area; many economic migrants work in formal jobs in public or private institutions, or as unskilled workers in different areas in the capital, all of which require daily movement outside Al-Baraka, through the core area (i.e. Wehda el Wataniya). This long journey, which requires using at least two means of transport, suggest that there are also other types of social network that can be built through working, by mixing with different people from other parts of the city.

Of course, it is difficult to tackle all the implications of these different social networks, although the obvious general implication is that the economic migrants place more emphasis upon their working neighborhoods relations than those with their relatives and follow ethnic people. When working and neighborhood relationships exist with people from same kinship or ethnic group, in this case the course of the relationship tends to take a different direction, including many other ethnic activities and actions. The reason for this is that neighborhood relations importantly include collective action to improve the quality of life in the shantytown, including planning the area, connecting it with water pipes and electricity, and establishing school and health facilities. All of these important issues arise and are communicated through the neighborhood network, while there is little prospect of achieving this through ethnic networks. In other words, the neighborhood collective identity develops and consolidates itself against the neighborhoods of other parts of the city; this demands commonality despite ethnic differences, and forming a kind of new shantytown collective identity. In the same line, working networks include collective arrangements to improve incomes, working conditions and benefits, which can be achieved through official means (e.g. unions, petitions) as well as informal ones, which provide information and ideas for action, and also place significant pressure upon employers.

This new shantytown identity differs from the rural-tribal identity, but is also not identical to middle class identity. It is geographically based primarily on southern and western Sudan in general. More precisely, it identifies the 'Al-Baraka people' or the 'Wehda el Wataniya people' against the rest of the city. This suggests that a new meaning of identity is developing through the residential experiences of the economic migrants.

4.5 Forced Migrants

The other general category of residents is the forced migrants, who came relatively recently to Khartoum, without preparation and with little preknowledge of the city, mostly having fled in groups from disasters or war zones. When they arrived, most initially depended upon their relatives in the capital, generally economic migrants who could manage to find permanent settlements on the periphery of the city after having been resettled from near the industrial areas. As many of these economic migrants also lived in squatter settlements near old planned areas, it was easy for them to host the newcomers in adjacent empty areas, which were being used as grazing land for Albatahin nomads who had been settling in the area, before the city gradually swallowed them.

These new arrivals' dependence upon economic migrant relatives was not only confined to finding a place to settle. It also involved finding jobs, learning the necessary skills of the city, and even obtaining direct financial support. In response, forced migrants tended to assume a lower social status than economic migrants. This was consolidated by the bureaucratic procedures of planning the area, where acquiring ownership and a place of residency in the area depended upon the time of arrival. Those who managed to arrive earlier enjoyed greater benefits. For example, the time limitation for the families to resettle in the area was decided as 1986, whereby any family that came after that and had the necessary other requirements (e.g. identity documents, marriage certificate, children birth certificates) had to resettle in another area called Et Tawidat (in Arabic: compensation), about five kilometers from Al-Baraka; others resettled in Dar es Salam in Omdurman. Even the specific places of settlement in Al-Baraka were determined by the time of residence, whereby older settlers stayed in their more central places while all those who came later had to move to other newer quarters.

While it seems more logical to give those who came first to Khartoum greater rewards, it also seems unfair to penalize the more vulnerable newcomers. This government policy is in line with its attitude towards the entire urban area, where older quarters and upper-middle class areas have always had the largest share of the city's cake.

The economic activities of forced migrants are usually attached to the informal economy, particularly because the city was involved in a deep economic decline when the waves of forced migrants started to find their way to the capital during 1980 to1990. This was due to IMF policies and political instability, until the National Islamic Front took power through a coup in 1989. This led the country into deeper economic crisis, accompanied by increased intensification of insecurity in the southern and western regions. This led to a further influx of IDPs towards the capital.

The steady increase of IDPs, with more people coming from Darfur and the Nuba Mountains, meant that the shantytowns became more heavily populated, and new shantytowns formed on the edges of the city. This led the old shantytowns and the markets in the core areas to be more prosperous, becoming an open arena for the thriving informal sector, while the houses in the old planned shantytowns emerged as valuable real estate.

The pressure from older migrants upon newcomers pushed the latter into keeping their original cultures in one way or another, perhaps to diminish the effect of economic migrant power. It appeared as if the only source of power acquired by forced migrants was their strong affiliation to their original areas, whereby through idealizing their traditions they might be able to match the power of economic migrants, for example through rhetoric like the idea that new migrants are not yet spoiled by the city's 'bad values,' and retain their loyalty to their ancestors. On the other hand, these traditions were also an integral part of the ideology of the economic migrants, which they used in interacting with outsiders in other parts of the city, or even when they communicated with other ethnic groups within the area. The presence of increasing numbers of forced migrants had other political benefits, giving ethnic groups more right to claim and gain more power, locally in the form of participating in bigger share from the dominant ethnic groups in the local committees, or in claims for more services for the shantytown as a whole from the government.

The economic hardships encountered by the forced migrants made them active in the informal economy, as it is the only economic arena in which the capacity for recruitment is unlimited, although the ability to gain success is very limited. Nonetheless, based upon their lack of other options, forced migrants continued to switch between informal activities. One such example is the recent expansion of gold mining, where thousands of people heard that it is very profitable, although very dangerous and hard, because the work places are usually in the desert areas. Nonetheless, people still circulate stories about lucky people becoming very rich after finding large chunks of raw gold.

Given that forced migrants are more attached to their original areas, and less adapted to urban life, they are more inclined to return home if it becomes more attractive or physically possible; for example, following the independence of South Sudan, the first among the southern people to return were the more disadvantaged people who came recently, who wished to go back to the south to resume their old life, which was interrupted by the war.

However, return seems like a benefit-loss calculation for forced migrants and economic migrants alike. Return to an original area is considered a better option for forced migrants, because they still have the connections and competence that can help them to resume their rural life there. By contrast, for economic migrants, they have already accumulated material assets and competences in the capital, and thus it is hard for them to abandon all of this. Subsequently, problems occur when there are no practical options other than returning to an original area, as in the case of the southern people. Perhaps here, changing their destination to a similar urban area would be an ideal solution.

The typical social networks of forced migrants center on kinship members and the ethnic group in the capital. Perhaps this is not very surprising, given their late arrival and their collective settlement together, or their dependence upon their kinfolk to find places to settle, and jobs. Forced migrants are generally more impoverished, which means that they are more dependent on informal activities, typically inside Al-Baraka or in Wehda el Wataniya market, with fewer contacts with other parts of the city.

Accordingly, the social networks of forced migrants include their relatives inside Al-Baraka area, as well as fellow tribe members in other shantytowns, in addition to their connections to their homeland; in fact, the forced migrants maintain stronger ties with the home areas, including for economic reasons, as they might receive some assistance from there such as agricultural products. Moreover, they depend upon their relatives in other areas in the town: sometimes, this becomes one way of surviving without money and work, by moving from one relative to another. This is more likely to work for a single person than an entire family. This also means that the dependence of newcomers upon their longer-resident relatives and friends is a considerable burden for economic migrants, who have limited resources and many needs. However, they endeavor to share what they have with their relatives, albeit with much hidden resentment - especially if the relatives belong to the wife's side.[24]

Forced migrants also try to build strong relationships with their neighbors, especially if they are not their relatives. This process take significant time, however, and more recently there are few collective challenges facing the whole neighborhoods to pull them together, given that all basic services and amenities are available; indeed, even the main function of the local committees has become confined to producing documents of residency and death certificates. Accordingly, the possibility of creating a strong relationship with neighbors lessens.

Forced migrants probably earn much more money in the capital than their home areas, although their expenses are also much higher. Most had lost all of their property before fleeing to Khartoum (Salih 2000), which means they started from a point of almost zero after their arrival in the capital. The implication of these limited social and economic networks is usually made tangible in the inability of the majority of forced migrants to generate sufficient income for their basic needs. While it might be easier for their children to find more opportunities, as their networks could grow with their age, it remains very difficult for latecomers to find ways to establish themselves, at least as the economic migrants have done in most cases. However, the second generation is more able to overcome these difficulties by sharing the same conditions and environment with the children of economic migrants.

In conclusion, the first generations of residents have gone through different life experiences that shaped their disparate accumulated competences. Through this, economic migrants have managed to secure more material and symbolic gains than forced migrants. Consequently, the meanings of being part of the shantytown and part of the first generation of settlers involves many differences between the two sub-groups, as well as many shared characteristics and experiences that justify categorizing all of them as one social group (e.g. the same lifestyle).

---

[24] Interview with Saymon, a tribal leader of the Shilluk in Al-Baraka, 16 June 2010.

Chapter Five: Educated People: Moving Towards the Middle Class

5.1 Introduction

This lifestyle group may be fewer in numbers, compared to the other two social lifestyles: nonetheless, it assumes a more powerful position and organizational role than either the first or second generation groups in the Al-Baraka area. Approximately speaking, the 'educated' lifestyle group includes all the people in the area who have acquired some kind of formal education, high-ranking jobs, or accumulated wealth. In the category of traders, literacy and formal education might not be as necessary or important, as with the case of many well-known traders.

There are some consistently specific materials and symbols that indicate belonging to this lifestyle group. Dress is one important symbol. The modern dress of trousers and shirt is dominant among male members of this group, especially at working times, when only traders prefer to wear traditional clothing (e.g. the *jalabia*, turban, and small traditional hat). By contrast, second generation youth also wear trousers and shirts or T-shirts, but usually in styles similar to hip-hop musicians, with big designs, bright colors, and many words and pictures on the T-shirts. This includes also importantly the mannerism of dropping the trousers down until underwear appears, which is called "system". While many first generation members also wear trousers and shirts when they are working, especially outside Al-Baraka or in their formal institutions, as soon as they return to their homes they switch to traditional dress. For 'educated' people, modern dress is their standard, though they might occasionally dress traditionally, albeit only for attending social events or for Friday prayers. Southern educated people mostly prefer wearing modern dress at all times.

Another distinctive practice for these educated people is using titles, usually the title of *Ustaz* (lit. teacher), or his community position, such calling him by his membership of local committees before the name, and sometimes his formal job (e.g. clerk), especially if it is high ranking. Using titles is not restricted to educated people: some members of first generations also enjoy using titles (e.g. sheikh, sultan, and *abuna* (lit. our father)), which can be used for ethnic or religious leadership positions. Nonetheless, the usage of titles to address educated people is more wide and seen as more legitimate, like using the title *saato* (lit. his excellency) for policemen, military men, and individuals who have high powered positions in the government.

The importance of these educated people comes from the high value attached by the community on formal education. This value clearly stems from the real experiences of the first generation of residents with local government and other parts of the city. This is because, since the arrival of the shantytown settlers to the city, all their urban experiences have been influenced by their relationships with formal urban institutions (local government). These relations were very hostile, with the government considering them as outsiders and a possible threat to the high urban standards of services in the capital during the 1960s to 1980s. At the same time, local residents of old quarters exerted significant pressure upon local government to eradicate the squatter settlements from their lands. This long story of bitter relations between the host community (urban) and the newcomers (pastoral/rural) produced an inferior position for the latter, and ironically also encouraged the desire on the part of the newcomers to gain the same position and privileges as the rest residents of Khartoum, as well as to defend themselves and protect their own interests. The first problem encountered by the squatter shantytowns at the time of settlement was the lack of schools, as well as all other services, which is why, from the beginning of constructing an area as a squatter settlement, the first kind of services that people wanted to install were schools for their children.

In a sense, having formal education meant having more urban experience and competence than the non-educated or less educated people (such as drop-out students). In this way, the community expected certain behaviors and attitudes from educated people, in terms of certain kinds of jobs and wealth. At the same time, educated people are offered more rewards and positions: "A candidate for membership in such a group has to qualify in two distinct fields. First, in the long, arduous, and costly battle for formal education and professional training; second, in acquiring through continuous socialization the dramaturgical skills and idioms necessary for partaking in the group's dramas and general symbolic activities its collective representations" (Cohen 1981: 217). Accordingly, having formal education becomes a resource in itself; this is why the majority of parents in Khartoum are trying very hard to educate their children, knowing that this is the only way to uplift their social position in the local community and the city as a whole. This is what has caused the number of private schools in Al-Baraka to exceed the number of public schools. How these educated people manage to assume more power and privilege than any other lifestyle group in Al-Baraka, as well as how they managed to take power specifically from the first generation after the upgrading of the area, will be the focus of this chapter.

5.2 Ceremony of Opening the New Stadium

After my arrival in Al-Baraka for my second fieldwork period in April 2010, I noticed a new football stadium being raised in the western part of the service area, locally called the green space, *al-saha al-khadra*. Notably, the new stadium is also green, both the main building and the pitch, and it is possible to see it from afar because three sides were fenced by long iron poles. While the service area is a large open space located in the heart of Al-Baraka designed to host all public services, it includes several buildings such as two private schools, a community center,[25] water well and temporal market.[26] Behind these buildings on the east side is a wide open area, including a field for football and an unfinished concrete building; usually, many people come to this area in the evening to drink local brewed beer *marîsa* and a more powerful liquor called *aragi*. To the west side of the area are two primary schools, one of which belongs to a church (now abandoned), as well as a huge new complex belonging to the police. Not far from this is a high building also belonging

[25] Started when the area was squatter settlement, then built with concrete materials (2000m^2) inside the service area in 1994 by DDR (a German NGO) and UNFPA, under the supervision of the Ministry of Social Planning. In its early years, the community center was used as a training centre for women's small business activities (e.g. sewing, soap making, midwives training, traditional artifacts, and literacy programs), and offered small loans and machines to the trainees, with a small shop to sell their products. Then a medical centre was added, which specialized in maternity services and children's vaccination, and a kindergarten. In 2002, the place was taken over by a Sudanese NGO related to the government, called Azza, which worked for some time in small business activities as well as micro-finance for women. Suddenly a dispute with the local administration over who controlled the centre escalated. Then Azza withdrew its funds and trainers (many of whom were women from Al-Baraka). Since then, the center has belonged to the Institution of Social Development, which promises to offer micro-finance projects to CBOs (community based organizations). Actually, no regular activities are going on, except some occasional events usually organized by local youth organizations; interview with Kany, the current director of the centre, 18 August 2010.

[26] Made of mud walls and roofed with straw, including cafés to watch satellite TV, play games and smoke shisha, other small places for tea ladies (women selling tea and coffee), and women selling food. The owners pay tax monthly to the municipal locality and the police (in case of cafés), though this is not considered as legal permanent ownership.

to a church, while in front of this, on the other side of the open space, are some informal homes. Behind this is another high fenced complex belonging to the security services, which seems like a permanent camp. The new stadium is located just behind this, and on the western edge of the area is a secondary school for girls.

It was surprising for many people that such a modern stadium would be built in Al-Baraka, with Eissa telling me that the government wanted to build it inside the service area, near the large market Wehda el Wataniya.[27] They chose to move the stadium to Al-Baraka because the government wanted to use it for hosting political events; this decision came from the governor of the locality (East Nile). Later on, I discovered that the funding for the stadium came from the Youth Association of Football and MTN, a communications company, whose social projects intends to build a football stadium in every locality in Khartoum state, for football teams belonging to youth league.

The opening ceremony of the stadium was in the afternoon of 13 July 2010. It was a huge ceremony, possibly the largest in the history of the Al-Baraka area, because it was attended by the president of Sudan, as well as several other ministers from the federal and state level, such as the minister of Youth and Sport and the governor of Khartoum State. Thousands of people from different parts of the capital—mainly belonging to youth league football—attended, alongside a few thousand local residents from Al-Baraka and other nearby shantytowns.

The ceremony started after the arrival of the president, who arrived a little late because several hundred youth footballers were lining the roads leading to the stadium; he arrived in an open-top car waving to the crowds. The program of the ceremony begun with a long reading of verses of the Qur'an, then the national anthem was played by national army musicians. The president and his entourage then visited an exhibition and some parts of the stadium, and subsequently sat in the main front stands. The program was presented by a famous sports radio presenter, in his very well known style. In the first part of the ceremony, many football teams passed in rows in front of the stands, followed by others on bicycles, then others riding horses. This was followed by a short football game for about half an hour between teams comprised of famous retired footballers who largely played for the two most popular clubs in Sudan, before a group of very well-known singers, both men and women, sung two songs praising the nation and the unity of its people. However, all

[27] Eissa is the secretary of local committee in Quarter No. 2.

sound system devices were directed towards the main upper level, where the officials sat in the western part of the stadium, while people on other sides, and those who had just climbed the fences or were watching from outside, were unable to hear clearly (see Figures No. 8 and 9). Therefore, most attendants were visibly bored and did not participate or react to the singing. The adjacent areas of the main upper level, which were filled by girls from secondary schools, made visible by their dresses, were apparently hearing the program and were involved. Eventually, the young military service trainees who were surrounding many parts of the football ground simply entered the pitch and came near to the main podium, which was located directly in front of the upper level of the stadium. This sudden move seemed to confuse the organizers, possibly preventing them from continuing their program as planned. Subsequently, four officials gave long speeches, starting with the governor of the locality, then the minister of youth and sport, followed by the governor of Khartoum state, then the president, whereby each official introduced the subsequent speaker, with singing before the last two speeches. The theme of the songs was praising bravery and masculinity, in the same kind of music usually broadcasted on the official radio and state TV, originally part of the folklore of Nile valley ethnic groups. The president danced to all the songs,[28] sometimes accompanied by his wife who sat beside him, while other officials occasionally also danced in front of their seats or moved towards the president, waving and praising. After the president's speech, the ceremony was over. There were crowds of photographers and TV cameras, and the event was broadcasted live on Khartoum state TV. There was a high security presence; indeed, it was noticeable that several snipers were monitoring the event from a building on the opposite side of the stadium. Overall, the ceremony took about one and a half to two hours.

The most obvious thing about the ceremony is that it was boring for the local people from Al-Baraka, given that I saw many people leaving the place early after the training soldiers entered the field ground. This was due to two reasons; firstly, the sound system devices were unable to let them clearly hear what was going on; and secondly, the various parts of the program were not interesting for local people; it was similar to what is consumed in formal public media, but not necessarily what local people enjoy. The music and songs performed in the ceremony were far

[28] In fact the president is well known for his interest in dance and this type of songs, with many of his critics on social media calling him "the dancing president".

removed from what local people usually hear in their parties or marriage concerts, or even in local rickshaws. The favorite music locally is usually African dance music, with heavy and fast beats accompanied by non-formal lyrics,[29] while some youths also listen to rap, hip-hop and reggae. The ceremony also lacked any kind of traditional dancing from southern and western Sudan, from which the majority of residents originated. Indeed, there are several traditional bands, perhaps for every single ethnic group, that regularly participate in such ceremonies. More-over, the ceremony did not include the types of local sports that are popular in the shantytowns, like Nuba wrestling, which is more popular than football. In conclusion, the opening ceremony was broadly alien for local people; rather, it was prepared and executed according to the taste of government officials and the culture of the middle class people who live in other parts of the city.

I also noticed that there were hundreds of people watching the ceremony from outside the stadium, from outside the fences directly or from some distance, including some people on from the other side of the road, all in the southern part of the stadium. This southern part is directly facing Quarter No. 4, and the majority of inhabitants in this quarter are from southern Sudan. They most likely decided to watch from a distance because they do not trust the police; indeed, there was a heavy presence of police vehicles and soldiers in the road between the stadium and the quarter. There were many large trucks full of heavily armed anti-riot soldiers, which clearly indicated expectations of protest from this side. For local residents, the police is their primary enemy, simply because they usually use brutal force against locals, as the area is famous for producing locally-brewed alcohol (e.g. *marîsa* and *aragi*) and there are many places where people from all over Khartoum come to drink. Even in the service area behind the new stadium, there is an open area to sell and drink local alcohol, usually in the afternoon. These activities are subject to frequent raids from the Public Order Police Department. It is not unusual to see large trucks belonging to police roaming the area at any time of the day. Another reason for local people declining to take part in this celebration was the fact that many southern people at that time had de-

[29] This type of music was originally called *agânî al-banât* (lit. women songs) in the past in formal circles in Khartoum, while people in shantytowns refer to it as *agânî tarab*, meaning enjoyable songs.

clared their affiliation and support of SPLA/M,[30] but perhaps they still wanted to know what was going on from a relative distance.

The day after the opening ceremony, I looked at one of the popular sports newspapers and found that coverage of the ceremony occupied almost a complete page, besides a prominent place on the front page accompanied by a picture of the president, his wife, and the rest of the officials when they entered the stadium at the beginning during the national anthem. On the page inside, there were many pictures of the ceremony, including two of the president. Other photographs included the minister of youth and sport during his speech, and the singers while they were performing, facing the officials while turning their backs on the rest of the audience. The eighteen singers were the most popular in the capital at the time, and it was very rare to see all of them in one place singing nationalist songs, which also indicates the huge amount of funds available for this ceremony. There was also a small picture showing parts of the crowd, and the content of the journalistic report mostly featured what the officials said in their speeches.

In the neighborhood in the evening, the ceremony was the main subject of conversation among young people in their usual sitting place at the station. Ali had attended the ceremony, and was very enthusiastic about the presence of the president and other officials for the first time in the area "*to see the mud houses.*"[31] He was also very happy to see the famous singers, and spent much time describing to other youth what had happened there. Meanwhile, Adam, like many others, had not attended, and he thought that the president would not be able to come and enter inside Al-Baraka. A few days later, I met Eissa and asked him for his view; he expressed his disapproval, because the organizers of the ceremony did not contact them as the local committee representing Al-Baraka. He thinks this was necessary because it was an opportunity for them to meet the president and other ministers to inform them about their problems and demands.

This event strongly symbolizes the relationship between Al-Baraka and the government on one side, as well as between Al-Baraka and the middle class areas on another side: one should not assume that the gov-

---

[30] The Sudanese People's Liberation Army/Movement the main political party representing South Sudan; at that time the party was sharing power in Khartoum according to the Comprehensive Peace Agreement of 2005, but still SPLA members declared their dissatisfaction with the ruling party of the north of Sudan.

[31] Ali is a teenager still studying at secondary level.

ernment and middle class people are identical, or that the government is simply representing them. Nonetheless, they share many characteristics, especially in terms of their relations with other peripheral entities (e.g. shantytowns, rural areas). While the government involves interconnected networks of bureaucratic offices organized in a hierarchal order, run by people largely drawn from the so called "middle class groups,"[32] at the same time not all middle class segments are necessary represented in the state, due to competition between various groups of political elites.[33]

In this regard, we could brush over the differences between the wide range of middle class groups and the government, and consider in this analysis both the government and middle class people as representing same ideology and actions towards shantytown settlers. In this way, we can interpret the policies and actions of the government and its agencies towards shantytowns as the way in which the entire rest of the city also views these areas. If this is the case, it is possible to imagine the sort of conduct and the program that was set for the stadium opening ceremony as reflecting how the government, and by extension the middle class people, look at shantytowns as being less valued and less developed, an arena for transmitting their knowledge and their worldview. Upon this basis, these elites assumed the power and authority to dictate and order what should be done and how things should be arranged. In this way, when the police and the organizers of the event set the way in which the event should unfold, this expresses deeper convictions of hegemony and denial of otherness in the area. That is why there were no efforts to know what local people liked to see, given that the local were not visible in the minds of the people who organized the event.

What is important here is the implication of such a perception inside the shantytown itself, because the presence of the government and middle class people' ideology and conceptions is not always transmitted through people who come from outside. Certainly, educated people from inside the shantytowns, who climbed the ladder of education and gained formal jobs and greater economic resources, can also be considered as part of the

[32] It is always difficult to define middle class people in the third world or global South. Nonetheless I use the term here in the same way as a "state class", which includes political elites and higher and middle level administrative staff who profit from state resources, and those in control of state resources and their allies (Neubert 2014: 31).

[33] Currently in Sudan, for example, the state is controlled by elites from the Nile Valley belonging largely to the Muslim Brotherhood party, who took power through a coup in 1989, but also a wide range of tribal leaders, businessmen, and religious elites allied with them.

middle class, which is the case in urban-rural relations everywhere in Sudan.

> "The barrier between school-educated professionals and farming population reflects the gulf between village populations and what farmers summarily call hakuma, that mythical agent of all good and all evil. The lack of self-confidence and determination which farmers seem to show in their dealings with Naas-al-Hakuma is not due to a lack of interest or expertise, or to the other bogey of urban experts, 'traditional mentality'. Rather, it is due to the expectation, backed by years of experience, that hakuma, and whoever represents it, wants to, and can only, be addressed by those who share its culture: school-educated, literate, cash-earning professionals. These are called in as mediators to deal with developmentalists, administrators and officials through ijtima'a oratory. As mediators, however, they may follow interests and objectives opposed to those of the farming population and the developmentalists; and thus, a cultural bias serves a social division which can frustrate and damage agricultural development" (Baumann 1981: 76-77).

The local educated people of Al-Baraka are part of the middle class by virtue of their life choices and practices, which seem similar in many aspects to other parts of the city. Even when there were disagreements, as in the case of not informing the local committee in advance about the event, the disagreement was rather about how the benefits and interests should be shared between the government of whole city and the "*government of the shantytown*"—as one of the leading members describes the local committee.[34]

I will continue this analysis of the educated lifestyle through looking at the local committee, as it represents their main vehicle for power and influences practiced at the local community level.

[34] Juma'a, interviewed in Al-Baraka, 28 May 2010.

Figure 8: Photo of the New Stadium ceremony 1
Large crowd at the beginning of the ceremony, unable to hear everything. Al-Baraka, fieldwork 2010.

Figure 9: Photo of the New Stadium Ceremony 2
The center stage set up in front of the president's seating, with crowds at other side of the field. Al-Baraka, fieldwork 2010.

5.3 Changing the Leadership of the Local Committees

In the election of the local committee for any quarter in Al-Baraka, there is usually a call for the quarter's residents to meet at a certain time and place. There should also be representatives of the locality, who are officially responsible for organizing the election. While those representatives are supposed to be neutral, in fact they are more likely to support the candidates of the ruling National Congress Party (NCP); accordingly, the distance between the government and the party is unclear or non-existent. For example, Saymon is the president of the local committee in Quarter No. 4 and the president of the National Congress Party in the quarter, with the majority of local committee members also members of the NCP. Most people do not differentiate between the government, local committees, and the NCP; indeed, they might use the three terms interchangeably. For all this, what is usually expected in every election is that the members of the NCP and the old local committee will win and continue running local affairs. What makes this likely to happen is the supervision of the locality's officials, including their ability to add five members to any winning list, which comprises ten members. Usually the added members are those who failed to be on the wining list through the direct votes from the NCP candidates list.

Sometimes if people are not satisfied with the performance of any local committee, they might try to change it. People are also sometimes dissatisfied due to the ethnic composition of the local committee, or they might assert that they have qualified candidates to fill the jobs from their fellow tribesmen. Therefore, sometimes more than one list might be introduced in the election, but usually because all different parties know that the NCP is able to impose its candidates through the specific regulation of the election and controlling the election process, usually even different candidates from different lists are drawn from the NCP. Moreover, people know that no one from outside the circle of the NCP can work effectively on the committee, because there will not be any support for them from the local government, especially if the person is seen as from a political opposition parties.

What happened in the last election of the local committee in Quarter No. 2 was remarkable, compared with the normal conditions outlined above. There was a new list introduced to challenge the main list of the old committee, which had been in position from the time of the planning of the area, and led by Awad, who is one of the oldest teachers in area and who currently has private schools at primary and secondary level. The new list was supported by the educated youth, who were not happy about the old committee, accusing them of being corrupt, taking the money from the water services,[35] and using land in public spaces for their personal benefit. Indeed, this view was shared by many other people in Al-Baraka, with Shiekh Ajab telling me that:

> "the ministry of settlements offered half of the cost of pipe network for the area, they offer all pipes, addition to that all wells were already there established by NGOs, with all that, they asked every house to pay 200 SDG, now there is a new well dug by the government. Still the water might stop for three days. They took all the money to their own pockets; because we know all of them we brought them to work in the local committees, when they started they have nothing now everyone owned a school. Awad took the land of his school, Taj took the computers brought by one NGO to educate local people, he used it later to have center for teaching computer."[36]

The group of young educated people was well organized; because many other people were dissatisfied with the old committee, they manage to secure enough votes for their list. However, the locality's officials refused this result, and after negotiation with the representatives of the other two lists, they agreed to take five members from every list. The educated youth thus partially managed to impose their candidates. However, after this, it become obvious that the majority of people were not satisfied with the work of the old local committee; the five old members included in the new committee, including Awad, withdrew themselves from active work on the new committee. Consequently, only candidates who were chosen by the young educated people became active members of the local committee.

Haroun was one of the educated youths behind this change. When I asked him about what happened, he said proudly:

> "Yagoub and Eissa came to the leadership of the local committee through revolution led by the young people. We were not happy about the old local committee led by Awad, because they transfer all the resources to their own private benefits, the land of the private schools owned by Awad originally located to be the local committee home. They collected from every house about 200 SDG as fees to connect the house to the water supply pipe. And

[35] The local committees control water services in Al-Baraka; they take about 10 SDG monthly and use the money to pay the cost of running the water wells (e.g. electricity, repair, technicians, networks).

[36] Shiekh (leader) Ajab is one of the first generation leaders; he was representing the local people at the time before the planning, then afterwards his power and authority diminished and was taken over by educated people. For this reason he was always criticizing the old local committee. Al-Baraka, 23 February 2012.

> they are all belonging to the ruling party (NCP). We took the opportunity of the last general assembly, we prepared a new list without their knowledge, and present[ed] it to the organizer of the assembly from the locality. Then the organizer were upset, because usually in such assembly, only one list would introduced, the one which belong and proved by the NCP, then they asked all different partied to agreed, then Awad return to be member of the local committee but he didn't work actively because he felt ashamed. Yagoub is a trusted man, he works in the security apparatus, he is known for refusing to take bribes. Now, the new local committee builds a new house for the local committee, they intend to build it to the second floor, they have surplus of money in the bank the only local committee in whole Al-Baraka area. It came from the monthly fees of water supply, 10 SDG from more than 1000 house in Quarter No. 2. Every member of the local committee has a job unlike other quarters, where you find the members are just working in the local committees."

When I asked Eissa about what happened in the assembly, to which he was unexpectedly elected, he told me a slightly different version:

> "The formation of the current local committee came with struggle between the old committee and the young people, because young people introduced suddenly their list of candidates, before that there were disagreements between old local committee with many local people because they accuse Fur people of being the dominant in the old committee. But the ruling party refused to recognize the new youth elected. At the end all groups agreed of forming a new local committee where it takes five from every list (there was a third list also). But then who actually take the real responsibility is the educated youth. They assured that every ethnic group is represented in the new local committee, so there are representation of Nuba, Southern, and kalmba. Even me I am a vice secretary of the committee originally, but then because of the absence of the elected one I replaced him."[37]

Educated people bear power and influence through certain institutions, and the physical presence of those institutions gives them important instruments. Places like local committee houses, schools or development centers are at the heart of these mechanisms used to achieve their leadership aspirations in the local community. This is why one of the important spaces to create at the time of the planning was the service area, which is always at the heart of any quarter and is large compared with other spaces. Moreover, the control of this open space is consistently prominent on

[37] Interview in Al-Baraka, 28 July 2010.

the agenda of local committees and local urban government, which indicates its real power in the shantytowns. This power was used to serve two purposes: firstly, the public one, which is the interest of the whole community; and secondly, the invisible one, which is the educated group interests. "It is this cultural process that transforms a category of people, like the members of a profession or the officials of a state institution, into a concrete, corporate, interacting, cooperative, and cohesive group. Its symbols act to unite, camouflage or mystify a major contradiction underlying the development and organization of elite groups generally, a contradiction between their universalistic and particularistic tendencies, between the duties of their members to serve wider publics and their simultaneous endeavor to develop their own sectional interests" (Cohen 1981: 216-217). These institutions also work as a hub for connections with outside powers, such as the central government and NGOs. Opening a new stadium or a popular police station is always welcomed by the educated, because it strengthens their power and enables them to host their own events, which symbolize their power and influence.

An important question is: why are educated people the majority in that committee, when they do not reflect the majority of the population in the area? The simple answer is because not everyone is interested in such a position; indeed, it is mainly educated people who are interested, since they know the importance of local committees and they consider themselves as part of 'the game.' This is even common in rural Sudan. Baumann's study in the Nuba Mountains clearly showed the position of formal meetings as an event controlled by educated elites:

> "An ijtima'a is usually called through the local sheikh or mujlis, and recruited on a village basis. It is hierarchically organized, separating a chairman and/or panel from the general public and/or audience. It is negotiated in Arabic which often tends to the literary, rather than the colloquial idiom. As the ijtima'a is formalized, so are the individual contributions which use formal openings, greetings, introductions, and which tend to stress general principals rather than to dwell on detailed technical points. An ijtima'a may thus be characterized as a village-based, hierarchically organized form of oratory. It is in this form that the farming population is expected to express its grievances, wishes and expertise. However, the ijtima'a is part of a school-educated, literate and hierarchical culture which is alien and intimidating to the farming population, and diametrically opposed to the values of their own culture" (Baumann 1980: 75).

The few other local people who came to these election meetings did so because they wanted to support their ethnic fellow members. Since tribal leaders did not compete in the election, because it was basically exclusively for educated people, usually very few numbers attended and voted in the election. When I asked local people about their views on the local committee, they usually explained that they saw them as not doing anything, or as corrupt people belonging to the government *hakuma*. Either way, ordinary people have very little interest in being part of the election process. For uneducated people, the local committee members—and perhaps the whole educated group—are just an extension of the government and other parts of the city in Al-Baraka. These locals punish the committee members through allegations of corruption, as well as commenting on their properties and wealth. Local people criticize local committee members publicly whenever possible, but such criticism is generally the same as their criticisms of the local government or police when they are dealt with unfairly. The only difference is that these local committee members are part of the community. On the other hand, people know that local committee members and other educated people are indispensable agents, without whom the government could not be handled. Thus their mediatory role is very important. Local committees issue all primary documents needed for further processes in other government offices; no one can receive plot ownership, nationality certificates, passports, driving licenses, etc. without an initial residence document from a local committee. This double relationship between local committee members and other local people is an expression of the domination-marginalization complex, whereby each side tries to use the other for his own needs, while simultaneously marginalizing them to curb their potential power.

From the perspective of local committee members and local educated people as a whole, it is clear from my many conversations with them that they assume that they are the natural leaders of their community, through their competence in dealing with the more powerful government and other parts of the city. Thus, they perceive that their power comes from their unique position, whereby they are able to deal with local people by being one of them and representing them, and at the same time by being part of the government and representing it at the local level. They see their power in their "hybrid" practices, and their ability to manipulate this "hybridity". Apparently, this seems true to a large extent: they are able to accumulate power and wealth through this process of manipulation of hybridity practices, whereby neither local people nor urban government are able to deal with each other without them.

Nonetheless, it is important to note the double marginalization implicit in the position of these local educated people. They are marginalized by local people, who view them as corrupt and belonging to the enemy (i.e. the government), and at the same time they are marginalized by the government and other parts of city, which views them as just part of the shantytowns. Meanwhile, all shantytown communities are stereotyped as at the bottom of the urban hierarchy. Consequently, local committee members and educated people are viewed at best as mere gatekeepers to reach that bottom level. Many of the contradictions and dispositions confirm this attitude from local committee members and educated people at large. They are well aware of how officials in their local government view them vis-a-vis other parts of the city, and how they are always the last priority for service delivery in the city. They are also aware of how other social groups in the area judge them. This double marginalization is consistently hidden by these educated groups, who assert the opposite, in their manipulation of "hybridity" practices.

Chapter Six: The Second Generation: Looking Outside

6.1 Introduction

The younger generation, who were born and raised in the shantytowns, construct their own, different lifestyle; due to their different circumstances and experiences, they have no strong attachment to a 'homeland,' or with other parts of the city. They have benefited from the availability of technology and modern materials to go beyond the national borders and the immediate environment around them. They are able to construct a strong connection with global youth cultures, usually selected and expressed via global media, which satisfies their needs and expectations of being different from their parents and their neighboring settlements in the city. Their choice of leisure practices as a means of constructing an alternative lifestyle is fitting with their age and world visions. Through rap and reggae, Congolese music, American and Indian movies, American wrestling and satellite TV, they have broadly re-invented themselves locally in the form of local dance music and rap-style dressing and behaviors.

Some earlier studies suggest that second generation migrants are characterized by being more assimilated to urban conditions; unlike their parents, they might manage to establish strong connections with other more affluent parts of the urban space. For example, Pauw's book *The Second Generation* is devoted to the town-born Bantu people in East London: these second generation people can, according to Pauw, be characterized as fully 'urban' or 'urbanized,' as their main social ties are all contained within the town, and urban modes of behavior are the only ones that count for them (Mayer 1971: ix). However, the case of the Al-Baraka second generation is entirely different, because the educated people could be considered more urbanized and assimilated to urban conditions, while second generation youths practice a totally different lifestyle to the rest of middle class areas in the city.

Another classic study conducted by Whyte in 1940s Chicago clearly established the distinctions between the second generation majority and the educated second generation minority in the American cities.

> "The younger generation has built up its own society relatively independent of the influence of its elders. Within the ranks of the younger men there are two main divisions: corner boys and college boys. Corner boys are groups of men who center their social activities upon particular street corners, with

> their adjoining barbershops, lunchrooms, poolrooms, or clubrooms. They constitute the bottom level of society within their age group, and at the same time they make up the great majority of the young men of Cornerville. During the depression most of them were unemployed or had only irregular employment. Few had completed high school, and many of them had left school before finishing the eighth grade. The college boys are a small group of young men who have risen above the corner-boy level through higher education. As they try to make places for themselves as professional men, they are still moving socially upward" (Foote 1981: xviii).

Certainly, the Al-Baraka second generation cannot be described as at the bottom of the social ladder, as the generation includes several different groups—as we will see—some of whom might be more affluent than other first generation and educated people. Nevertheless, gang members (*negarz*) might be considered as outlaws, and the most disrespected group in the Al-Baraka community.

The lifestyle of the second generation developed in certain spaces that are created and used exclusively by the youth, such the stations, shisha cafés, and music parties. These places are where youth meet, interact and share their practices through producing and using materials—such as electronic technologies—and associated skills. They are able to impose distinctive meanings onto their lifestyle. Studying those exclusive spaces is thus vital to understanding and analyzing the second generation's construction of their unique lifestyle and practices; this makes it possible to understand the dynamic processes of being part of the whole shantytown, and having a very distinctive way of life.

Generally, the first generation (the elders) are more accepting of the discriminatory measures enforced by the government and the rest of the city on Al-Baraka; they take this for granted, as a part of the overall urban environment. They came to the capital more recently than other settled populations, and, finding that they lacked the qualifications and skills of middle class groups, saw it as inevitable to live on the periphery of the city. Economic migrants experienced low status discrimination through their working experiences and their low employment grades. Forced migrants came even later, without seeing the capital as their natural new home, and saw no possibility of claiming any kind of power and equality. In other words, the first generation seems more accepting of the lower status given to them by the government and middle class residents, while educated people and the second generation show many signs of refusal of this status, and sometimes resistance to it. Their refusal is found-ed on an opposition to the views and practices of the first generation. While children-parent cooperation is not always the case, one must consider that disagreement may occur in the family. When it happens, conflict usually takes two forms: first, when the children/youth begin to assert themselves, especially during adolescence; and secondly, intergenerational disagreement, which essentially involves differences in opinion and practices. When youngsters try to disregard traditional values and standard rules of conduct, elders regard such practices as deviant behavior. At the same time, the influence of urbanization is noticeable in the occupational, educational and income differences between parents and children/youth, since most parents migrated from rural areas when they were adults, with little formal education, due to which they acquired low paid occupations. On the other hand, youth have had access to higher and better educational facilities and better informal jobs, and thus higher incomes. This might cause conflict, since children have more educational qualifications and better urban competence than their parents (Bannaga 1987: 97-98).

For the second generation, other parts of the city are where they feel inferior, which is expressed through different mediums, the most obvious of which relates to material resources. These differences are expressed in house designs and buildings, available services, and forms of entertainment. These differences are more exposed to young people who have consistent engagements with other parts of the city, usually through education. Given that the secondary schools in Al-Baraka and other shantytowns are not big enough to accommodate all students (especially schools of higher quality) at present, many of the students need to study in other parts of the city. This has always been the case, because shantytowns are the last areas to receive education and other services and facilities. Older generations of educated people informed me that most of their education was in other areas. This compulsory contact with other affluent parts of the city generates a sense of inferiority, although the reaction to that challenge might differ between individuals. Some young shantytown settlers use their agency and opportunity, and advance in their studies to reach higher education and join the educated lifestyle; many others have chosen to drop out from formal education and try their luck in other fields of employment.

6.2 The Party

One day in September 2010, I went with Ali to attend a marriage party in Quarter No. 1, of a relative of one of Ali's friends. The party started immediately after sunset, and the performers were a big band, called *'wtar eljebal* (lit. Strings of the Mountains). The mountains here refers to the Nuba Mountains, where the Morgi people—the ethnic group of the wedding family—come from. The band was made up of about fifteen dancers and ten musicians, beside one singer, who also played *tambour*, a kind of traditional stringed instrument like a mandolin. Other musicians played various kinds of drums, one played electric guitar and another a tambourine. All dancers appeared in very colorful clothes, with many traditional accessories, and they were the first to start the dancing, before many people followed. The language of the songs was Nuba, with many different languages to accommodate all the different Nuba Mountains ethnic groups. Soon, the large open space filled with dancers, organized in circles moving slowly, where older people lined up together, followed by older women and younger people, with the children at the end. The majority of the dancers were from the older generation, above thirty, largely married (from their dresses, especially the women). The dancing was very emotional, as people remembered the homeland with many joyful expressions. Many other people, especially the young and those from other ethnic groups, remained watching and listening. This continued for about two hours without a pause, from one song to another until the evening prayer call came from a mosque located in the same open space. Subsequently, many people left the place, many of whom seemed to come from other parts of the city, while others stayed chatting.

At about nine o'clock, the second part of the wedding party started, this time featuring a keyboard musician with one female singer and many sound system devices. Then the bride arrived with celebrations from their relatives. The singing started with a slow rhythm, with songs called "women songs," usually considered as part of the marriage ceremony.[38] With these songs, only the bride and bridegroom were dancing with their close relatives and friends, and increasingly more young people. Then faster rhythm songs started, locally known as *tarab* songs, which developed from the earlier women's songs in terms of the melody and lyrics. The tune also incorporated more varied sounds and effects, and seemed

[38] In the past this was performed by women alone to celebrate marriages, accompanied by drums, in northern Sudan and big cities.

to also borrow from rap and hip-hop music. When these songs started, hundreds of young people entered the dance floor. They were very skilled in certain dance styles and moves, with all of them bending or jumping. The songs were written in the normal daily language of shantytown settlers, which is a mix of urban Arabic with vernacular languages: these songs are generally called *agânî habit* (lit. low quality singing). This is very different from formal Arabic or urban Sudanese languages, which are usually used in public media songs. For example, one song was titled 'my lover is without money,' and 'another lover will come.' Although the subjects of the songs are not necessarily very different, mostly about romance, the way in which they are expressed differs between direct language or not urban standard language.[39] The songs are also performed in different ways; this was a very interactive performance between the singer, musician and dancers. In every song, there were certain words used repeatedly, whereupon the dancers and listeners responded with loud screaming and more spectacular movements. These words were varied, with some based upon ethnicity: in every song there was mention of the Morgi (the groom's ethnic group), the Nuba (the larger ethnic group), the Fur (the largest ethnic group in the area), and westerners (people from western Sudan). Based upon the area were the words Karton (the former name of the area before re-planning), Al-Wehda (the name for all shantytowns, and the oldest planned quarters), Haj Yousif (the largest area of the city, which includes other middle class areas beside the shantytowns), and Ombadda (the area of Omdurman city that also includes large shantytowns). Then there were words based upon football: Alhilal (the most popular football club in Sudan), Almarikh (the second largest club in Sudan), and Sadomba (the name of a famous football striker at that time from Zambia). Then for the policemen: Sharg Al-nil (the police department in the locality), and Alrasa (the headquarters of the police). Each name was proceeded by the word *nas* (lit. the people of). Finally, the singer also mentioned many personal names, including the groom's, and then her friends and companions. At the end of every song, the musician usually engaged in a long solo where the rhythm reached its height, and the dancing became more frenzied. This happened most in the final song, where the solo was far longer and hotter, and by the end of it many youngsters had taken out their machetes and were waving them in the air whilst dancing.

[39] Sometimes the language of shantytowns settlers, especially the younger generations, is described as street language.

Until that time, I had been informed that only gang members hold machetes,[40] but because there were a large number of machete-holding dancers I subsequently started to investigate the nature of these gangs. I was worried after the party, which finished after eleven o'clock,[41] because I thought trouble was brewing with all the machetes in the hands of those young people, but what happened was the opposite. The youth divided into small groups chatting together, before each group started to move towards its home destination. Through chatting with some of them, I discovered that many of them were students in secondary schools. They were mostly normal young people who developed social relationships with their peers from the neighborhoods or schools. While through my conversations with first generation people and educated people, I gained the impression that all the youth who hold machetes and live in closed groups are part of the *negarz* gangs, through this party and many other experiences I started to think about this issue differently. Firstly, there were a number of gang groups that might engage in criminal activities inside and outside the shantytowns, such as looting and robberies. They have certain rules inside their groups, including the refusal of all traditional social norms, like normal family ties and special relationships with parents. In this sense, the first rule of these gangs is to replace all normal social ties with the gang members and leader. This is the root of the antisocial behavior of the *negarz* gangs. They also tend to form their ways of spending time together, not believing in having stable jobs or any normal social commitments.[42]

However, the majority of youth who own machetes and formed small groups in their neighborhoods are not practicing that formal type of gang lifestyle; rather, they simply hang out in their stations to spend their leisure time together. Having a machete is a kind of weapon to protect themselves, rather than using it to commit criminal activities. Because they are living with their families and go to schools or work in the market, this means that the community has some kind of authority over them. However, this creates confusion between the gang members and other neighborhood groups, causing strained relations between the second and

[40] Gangs were locally called *negarz* (referring to the word Negro) in line with rap and hip hop music references, because gang members use famous African American singers as their heroes, and usually try to dress like them.

[41] The official time for ending parties in the capital.

[42] This information was gathered from different sources and at different times, some through direct observations in the neighborhoods.

first generation and the educated people, in the sense that second generation youths fall victim to generalized judgment from the two other lifestyle groups. Moreover, because those two lifestyles are more powerful in the community, they are able to place significant pressure upon young people. It is true that the voices, practices and vision of young people themselves are still waiting to be heard and considered locally. We know remarkably very little about them. Children and youth, in African shantytowns as elsewhere, have often remained 'silent others.' They are often viewed and judged from the outside and from above as a 'problem' or a 'lost generation' (De Boeck 2005: 2).

6.3 The Station (*al-Muhatta*)

The station is where the youth meet and interact, as well as learning from each other, and where they establish their distinctive lifestyle, and recognize their power and ability to make a difference. Therefore, the station is at the heart of the second generation's construction of their unique lifestyle, where it is possible to visualize the vibrant and dynamic processes of being part of the whole shantytown, and having a very distinctive way of life. This is because the station is an inclusive space for youngsters. While it is of course public, usually just part of the street or near to a shop or football ground, nonetheless, it is always occupied by young people, usually throughout the whole day. Sometimes, there are few or no youngsters, especially during the school day, but generally in the evening you can find it full of one or many groups of chatting youth. It is also a meeting point where young people come to find others, where they go to play games or go to the large market, or even to gather to have dinner (see Figure No. 10).

In my neighborhood during my first fieldwork period in Quarter No. 2, the station was in front of my house. Directly opposite my door was the shop of Adam, in front of which there was a verandah made of wood and straw and covered by empty sacks. Inside there were two large tables, used for some time for selling vegetables and meat in the morning, but since the school opened its doors, the young man who run this business has stopped working.

One Friday in July 2010, I heard a loud noise from the direction of the shop. After some time, I came to ascertain what had happened. Adam told me that the owner of the shop had come and argued with the youth who were there at the time, asking them to leave the place and not sit on the tables. Because he was nervous, the argument escalated and he insulted the young people there, describing them as useless and as naughty children. Some of the youngsters shouted back at him, then other older people intervened, and the young people agreed not to come back and sit on his tables.

The next evening, I went outside to find the youngsters sitting beside the wall of my house, with no one sitting on the tables, while Adam was sitting alone on the ground in front of his shop. Adam told me that the owner had asked him to prevent any youngsters from sitting on the tables, but he did not like to do that because he thought that if the owner wanted to keep his tables without damage, he should take them to another place; being on the street in an open verandah made them public property, and thus everyone had the right to sit on them. He also did not like the way in which the owner had talked with the youth, using offensive words, and he described him as a bad man. In the coming two days, the same thing happened; Adam preferred to sit inside his shop alone, while the youngsters kept sitting under different walls in the street.

On the third day, I came out and found Adam sitting on an empty sack on the ground, and I sat beside him before one of our neighbors came, and we started chatting.[43] The neighbor then sat on one table; he is not usually in the station, so he was not aware of the problem. No one told him, and after a while, another person called Yahia, the nephew of the shop owner, came.[44] He was renting one part of the house where the shop is located. Yahia also sat on one table, despite being aware of the problem, but maybe because he considered himself as not part of the youth or because the owner is his uncle. After some time, Bashir came and also sat on one table. Bashir is one of the youth's unofficial leaders, always very active and talking. The whole conversation then became about the ban on sitting on the tables. While Yahia and Adam agreed on the right of the owner in preventing the youth from sitting there, while Bashir insisted that they also have the right to sit there, and the place is their station, where no one can stop them. Soon, many other youth came and sat on the tables while the conversation continued—in a rather funny way, because even Yahia and Adam were not totally convinced by the views of the owner, and also they enjoyed sitting with the youths all the time. Actually, the relationship between the youngsters and Yahia and Adam was very good, with them sharing many things together. There is a

---

[43] He is working in building sector he rented the other side of my house, and he was living with his brother.

[44] He is a graduate from university, and had joined the air force as a trainee at that time.

mutual respect at least in their interactions, although Adam and Yahia are not involved in all the activities of the youth when they go to other places from the station (for playing, eating, and dating); regardless, though, they share views and knowledge together.

Since that time, the youth started to come as usual to the tables, and no one talked about the incident. It seems like everybody involved, even the owner, was convinced that there was no way to prevent the young people from sitting there, and because other people involved—like Adam and Yahia—accepted the presence of the youth, and even considered themselves, in some regards, as part of the station.

This incident indicates the contests between different generations and different social groups. For the second generation, creating their own space is a very strategic goal; indeed, it is a part of the identity of the group, because without an inclusive space where members can communicate and perform their activities freely, there would not be any sense of group solidarity. In contrast, for the first generation and the educated group, the youths represented a certain category of the community, and should follow certain steps in their behaviors and practices in order for them to be socially accepted and successful young people. For the first generation and the educated people, this means that ideal practices for youngsters should be performed in their homes and their schools, and they should follow what their teachers teach them in the schools, and what their parents teach them in their homes. This view is held more firmly by the educated group, through copying it from middle class culture, whereby children and youth are usually perceived as separate to adulthood and as 'people in the process of becoming rather than being'. They are depicted as dependent, immoral, and incapable of assuming responsibility, properly confined to the protection of family and school. This concept developed among the middle class in Europe and North America, and has been successfully globalized, whereby youth who do not fit this picture are considered either at risk or posing a risk to their society. Parents who do not follow these idealized Western-style child-rearing practices are seen as irresponsible and corrupt (De Boeck 2005: 3). As a result, the first generation and the educated people are aware that if these youth manage to create their own space (the station) outside of these two ideal spaces, this would endanger the ideal life cycle that is prepared for young people to follow throughout their lives.

In the month of Ramadan,[45] neighbors usually sit together chatting after breaking the fast, including different groups and generations. One day, the conversation was about the station, with all older people and the educated sharing the view that the station is a very bad place, and the main reason why students failed in their studies. For them, the stations are the places where young people learn to be naughty and disobedient. The few youth who attended kept silent, not for approval but out of respect for the elders, and maybe because they were the minority and apparently the most powerless. Certainly, with the varying experiences and occupations of the younger generations, differentiations have begun to occur among a previously homogeneous first generation population. This has had a great effect on the degree of intimacy in relations in the neighborhoods. As younger generations have begun to develop different styles of life, they have developed different meanings from the older generations (Bannaga 1987: 103). However, this is not always the case, in the sense that the youngsters also have the option of protesting through not having any social contacts with other generations and other social groups, as in the case of the gangsters, although that made them prey for all kinds of punishments and bad reputation.

There are examples of young people managing to contest other generations and social groups without being forced to leave the community or avoid other people, as in the case of rickshaw drivers. These drivers maintain many of the behaviors and activities of youth, and might display these in front of other groups without fear, simply because they are independent financially, or even better off than other groups. In the same Ramadan at one time, two elders came up to Sabery and asked him, in a very serious way, why his younger brother did not pray with them after breaking fast on the street.[46] Sabery replied - in an embarrassed tone—that it was his choice, and they would have to go and ask him about his behavior. The elders were silent; they could not talk with Hassan, apparently because they knew that he would not care about them, as he was always outspoken about his freedom and disregard for anyone's views of social mores. In fact, the elders came to Sabery because they knew that he respected traditions and older people, and were pushing him to put pressure on his young brother. Apparently, that did not succeed for the

---

[45] A holy month, where Muslims fast during the day, and local people break the fast together on the street.

[46] Sabery is a rickshaw driver who owns two rickshaws, and his younger brother Hassan also owns two rickshaws.

simple reason that even Sabery has no authority upon his younger brother.

Another alternative to the station in the neighborhood is the PlayStation shop (see Figure No. 11). The shop is very small one; in fact, it was not originally a shop, but a few meters taken from the street by the owner and constructed into a booth with temporary materials.[47] Inside, there are two large TVs and two PlayStations, with four chairs in front of them and more chairs behind for the viewers. Outside, there was a woman selling snacks for children and young people. Youth and children usually meet inside the shop or immediately outside it. Children typically come to play the games, while the older and more experienced players sit in the chairs behind to help the children. The most usual game is football. At first, there are options for the players and teams; sometimes the more experienced youth might play the whole game for the younger children, after helping them with the initial options. The older youths were actually controlling the shop with the help of the owner, but their cooperation with the children did not seem satisfying to them. Thus some may prefer to sit in the station near Adam's shop, because there they have the chance to be around people of their age, or older than them. They may also be able to find some new experiences there, besides being more independent from the influences of their families.

6.4 The Shisha Café

Another place where young people can hang out in the Al-Baraka area is in the southeastern part of the service area, where there are several cafés, some for watching satellite TV, some for playing games (e.g. cards, dominoes) and others for smoking shisha and watching TV channels. The latter type is the most popular, as increasing numbers of young people enjoy smoking shisha. Usually every group of friends goes there, or regularly meets there at certain times.

I visited one place several times and interviewed the owner of the café. While the TVs are only for entertaining the smokers, many young people come to the place just to watch the two TVs set up in the café because there is no charge for watching them, unlike other watching cafés. Sometimes, the owner might ask some of the youngsters who was sitting there for long hours to leave the place, and give the seats to people who

---

[47] The owner is also young man still in secondary school, and built the shop in front of his house as a personal enterprise.

want to smoke shisha. The large TV usually showed music videos from CDs in the morning, especially Congolese music and rap, hip-hop, and reggae music,[48] then in the afternoon they put American movies on, before switching to action movie channels in the evening. The smaller TV showed Aljazeera news in the morning, usually enjoyed more by older people, as there are many of them who come to smoke shisha. From the afternoon onwards, this TV was switched to Indian movie channels, continuing until the café closed its doors at midnight.

Sometimes, what should be watched on the TVs became a contested issue, when some of the youngsters wanted to watch a certain CD or specific type of music, while others disagreed. The owner sometimes became more aggressive with the bad youth, and might even throw them out. The problem usually came from regular customers who came on a daily basis to smoke shisha, because that gave them the advantage over others, in terms of choosing what they wanted to watch.

However, the most interesting thing was that nothing produced in Sudan or by official media was shown on the TVs at any time. Even the music videos of singers who were broadly famous in the shantytowns were not shown. Thus, all types of media entertainment consumed in those cafés were globally produced. Even in other watching cafés, the main viewings were European football and American wrestling, beside the same content as mentioned above. Indeed, through such communication with global popular youth cultures, two main attitudes are developing.

Firstly, the distance from the cultures broadly held in the shantytown environment becomes greater. These cultures represent the traditional, maintained and disseminated by the elders, as well as middle class culture disseminated through official media (e.g. radio, government TV). For traditional culture, its position becomes weakened because the social environment is so very varied, and the younger generation has no experience within their homeland to develop any meaningful links with traditions. As for the official middle class culture, it is not suitable to conditions in the shantytowns, as it is mainly made by and for middle class people. Elements of formal culture are just not feasible for the shantytown settlers, even in the educational curriculum, which makes the contents of this middle class culture mostly irrelevant and out of touch for young people.

---

[48] Those three kinds of music are locally called *negarz* music, the term derived from the word Negro (which was usually used in the songs to describe African-Americans).

Secondly, attachment to global youth culture has intensified. The more that young people have been exposed to global youth culture, the more it has apparently influenced their perceptions and worldviews. Naturally, this is a very straightforward outcome, which is evident from the increasing participation of young people in gang groups, whether in the more criminal versions or the neighborhood versions. This is further demonstrated through the social alienation of young people and their tendency to exclude themselves from other lifestyles groups. Through creating their own spaces and arenas of interaction, youth are able to consolidate their own specific lifestyle and their distinctive way of practicing their life.

Figure 10: Photo of Young People 1

Young men creating their own space (the station), Al-Baraka, fieldwork 2011.

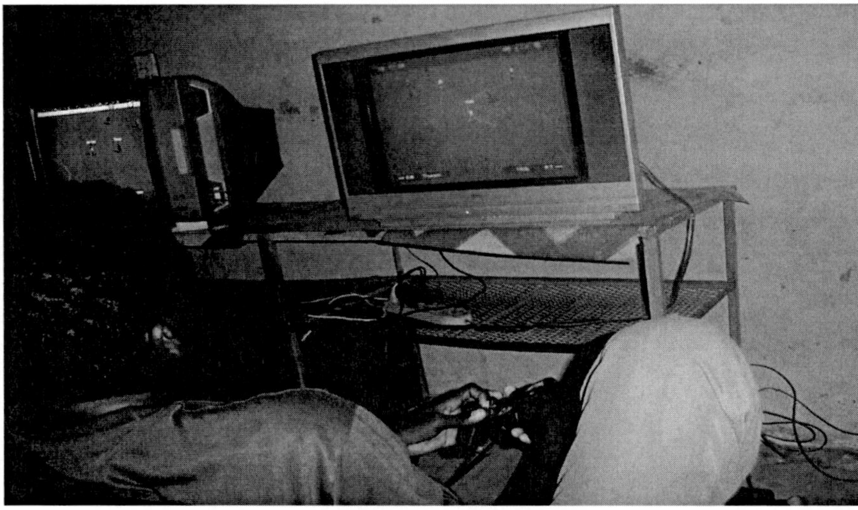

Figure 11: Photo of Young People 2

Young people playing on a PlayStation, establishing a strong relationship with technology, fieldwork 2011.

Chapter Seven: The Localization Process

7.1 Introduction

One of the important questions that we need to deal with here is whether people really choose their way of life, or if they obtain it from their surrounding environment. As the empirical data indicates, there is a trend of agency among people, in a sense that even among young people it is not hard to find some traditional cultures, or someone more attached to a middle class lifestyle more than a global youth lifestyle. Certainly, there is some personal agency at play, although we should not exaggerate this, given that this has its own limits, particularly within the realm of the three options of the triangle in most cases.

The second question is, then, how are people able to choose? Moreover, what are the processes and dynamics of this selection? Certainly, the willingness of people, and the influences of those around them, play a major role, as well as the entire structure of the community, and the options available to everyone, in terms of determining a person's *actual* identity (practiced) and their *verbal* identity (ethnic). We should note here the distinction between the *actual* identity, namely the identity expressed by the behavior of the people and their daily life routines, and the *verbal* identity, namely the identity expressed by the people themselves, but one that does not necessarily fully represent their behaviors; indeed, the importance of this distinction is that it shows the discrepancies between social influence and agency. While *verbal* identity represents an imposed identity, or what the community expects you to define yourself as, according to community values, the *actual* identity represents the will of individual people and their personal choice according to experience. Of course, not all community members are caught in a trap of contradictions between the two types of their identities.

If people are able to use their agency to choose and move between different lifestyles, then the question might then be, how do those three lifestyles exist in the everyday, as well as how they found their way into the realm of the shantytowns. This was apparently through the existence of diverse kinds of institutions, activities and values, whose origins we can trace to the homeland, the rest of the city, or to globalized youth culture.

Indeed, if we are to understand how this complex set of lifestyles coexists together and how they are influencing and imposing meanings onto the lives of local people, we might need to better understand the directions of social change that exist in the shantytowns, through using the concept of a localization process. The localization process enables different sets of activities, institutions, and values to find their way into shantytown social life. Through gradual processes of localization and domestication, this moves these social practices from being exclusively introduced and used by a minority in the extreme corners to towards the center, where increasingly more people can accept it or become part of it. In order for this to happen, many changes and modifications need to be incorporated to the original idea. Accordingly, we will try to illustrate three examples drawn from the three social lifestyles that dominate in the shantytowns.

The concept of a localization process seems vital to understanding and ascertaining how local people adopt different kinds of behaviors, institutions and activities from various origins and re-inventing them locally to be their own, thus removing any sense of alienation. The concept has been extensively used in recent years to understand the nature and direction of social changes, but mainly to explain how Western modernity penetrates other cultures as "yet another attempt to accommodate cultural particularity, which acknowledge[s] the fact that people across the world share similar predicaments and dreams regarding modernity, [and which] can be found among those who explore the idea of the existence of 'alternative', 'other', 'local', 'parallel', 'multiple' modernities different from the West" (Geschiere 2008: 2).

Another set of concepts is widely used to explain how materials and technologies are changing in the hands of 'end-users,' or by the requirements of the consumer's different environment, including appropriation, innovation, modification, creativity and technological diffusion. These terms are widely employed by the Diffusion of Innovation School, led by the sociologist Everett Rogers (Beck 2009: 161), Science and Technology Studies (STS), and the Social Construction of Technology (SCOT). Other studies have shown that a radical technological transformation also occurs in different local communities with imported technologies and ideas. This is clearly demonstrated in the example of the appropriation of the Sudanese truck (*sifunja*), where "the appropriation of the TJ [Sudanese Bedford trucks], as well as the appropriation of a host of other artifacts handled by users in a manners not intended by the manufacturer, should be regarded as more akin to reinvention" (Beck 2009: 162).

The advantage of using the concept of a localization process is in its ability to include a wide array of ideas, activities and social practices drawn from various sources. This means that the focus is on the process of the transformation itself, rather than on which source it relates to, and to which sections of the population. In this way, people can recruit ideas and activities from the homeland, such as for example Nuba wrestling, which was re-invented by adding different features and local aspects, some of which came from the urban environment, and some from traditions of other ethnic groups or from global media. Eventually, it has become the most popular sport in the area and very successful financially and socially. People also adopt modern education from the urban neighborhood, and adjust it to local needs, into very successful enterprises for graduate people; a private school can be a normal house constructed from cheap materials, but it can often help a local student to get the best results in the whole capital city. All these inventions come from different sources, but are passed through certain processes to become considered part of the local scene. It is broadly started by a specific lifestyle group, then gains more acceptance from other lifestyles, through long processes that do not always end with success, like rap culture, for example, which is still confined to a certain lifestyle (the youth).

Through these processes, certain elements become removed from the original activity, and certain modifications are added through the collective works of many other lifestyles groups until it reaches the point of being accepted as a local activity, although any project of localization has the risk of delay or failure. This localization process is very dynamic and needs serious efforts and careful management to gain the approval of different social groups in the community; thus no single lifestyle group has the authority to give this approval. Certainly, mutual acceptance and recognition can qualify any activity to be viewed as successfully localized, as we will see in the coming three detailed examples.

7.2. Nuba Wrestling

Nuba wrestling was introduced in the capital around 1975, in the Hamed Elnil area near to a famous Sufi shrine and cemetery, adjacent to Ombadda shantytown in Omdurman city.[49] Then in the 1980s, another arena for

---

[49] The city of Omdurman, situated on the western banks of the Nile, is the national centre of commerce and the largest city in Sudan. Between 1885 and 1898 (the Mahdist era), Omdurman became the capital and the major economic and political centre. How-

wrestling started to dominate, located in Wehda el Wataniya near to a large market, where many groups of Nuba Mountains people were living in several shantytowns surrounding the market. Gradually, the arena of Wehda el Wataniya became more successful, with huge numbers of fans following the wrestling on a weekly basis, while wrestling in Hamed Elnil started to decline, mainly because nearby areas surrounding the Sufi shrine became parts of first and second class settlements.[50] The real motivation for those Nuba Mountains people to practice wrestling was to maintain one of their homeland traditions, as many of them had practiced wrestling in the Nuba Mountains when they were young. Accordingly, the rules and ceremonies that accompanied the wrestling at the beginning were just as they had learnt in their home areas. Even the divisions between wrestlers were organized according to the ethnic groups to which the members belonged, while older ones became responsible for training and financing the wrestling. Nyamang, Angolo, Dilling, Talodi, Hadra, and Hawazma are some of the ethnic groups that are considered as the basis for wrestling groups.[51] What made the wrestling very successful in Wehda el Wataniya was the increasing numbers of people who followed it every week. These people were not only from the Nuba Mountains: in fact the majority were from other ethnic groups which did not practice wrestling in their home areas, which is surprising because Nuba Mountains people are the third largest ethnic group in the shantytowns (see Figure No. 12).

In the Nuba Mountains (the home area), wrestling is practiced after the harvest in certain places, where every clan brings its best fighters as a part of the harvest festivity, which also includes marriages, rites of passage, etc. People who experienced wrestling in the Nuba Mountains include the majority of first generation individuals, who usually engaged in the wrestling as organizers and fans.[52] Some of the wrestlers still move between the capital and Nuba Mountains, because they are brought to the capital by the clubs solely to take part in the wrestling, and they have no

---

ever, from 1898 to 1956, the Anglo-Egyptian Condominium rule re-instated Khartoum as the capital and the main trade and cultural centre (Abdalla 2008: 31).

[50] This area is called Elmohandeseen (the Engineers) and is nowadays considered as one of the very expensive first class areas in the capital.

[51] The Hawazma ethnic group lives in the Nuba Mountains, but considers itself as Arab in origin; however, they still borrow wrestling traditions from their Nuba neighbors.

[52] This group includes association members, club managers and members, referees, trainers, and people who organize the wrestling in the arena (e.g. selling tickets, keeping order inside the arena).

families or jobs in the capital. Those groups of home-practicing wrestling usually described to me on different occasions that wrestling in the Nuba Mountains is a more "natural" and richer experience, which includes the whole clan, whereby the wrestler becomes the symbol of strength and honor of his people. Accordingly, the wrestler becomes the focus of the whole community, and the older experienced people (*sabara*) take responsibility for everything related to the wrestlers, beginning from his daily food and training sessions to his time management. On the day of wrestling, all clan members come to support their fighters, women sing and chant to encourage their boys, while traditional horn instrument *garen* and drums are used to celebrate the tradition. Wrestlers decorate their bodies with ash, *suksuk*[53] on their wrists and necks, and amulets on their arms and thighs. Based on this atmosphere, the wrestlers become as crazy and frenzied as their relatives who support them. However, this is not all existent in the wrestling of the capital, or at least not in the same way, or more precisely not with the same motivations. While in the Nuba Mountains, people fight for the pride of the clan and to prove its power and bravery, in the capital wrestlers fight for money and the enjoyment of the fans, who do not belong to one ethnic group or even one residential area in the shantytowns. Other differences accounted by home area practitioners were that the wrestling in the Nuba Mountains is a more free experience, with far less rules and obligations, with no need for registration, putting them in different categories, or prohibition of certain dangerous attacking methods, as is the case in the capital.

In the early 1990s, an assistant medical doctor who was involved in the organization of wrestling arena of Wehda el Wataniya in the large market convinced others to organize wrestling inside a large tent and charge fans for watching it, whereby the revenue was divided between the groups. The idea worked well, and others added more ideas; indeed, soon people agreed to set up a wrestling association and change the clan-based groups to sport clubs, which prompted their change of names. The first club to appear was Sagr Al-Gedian, named after a type of hawk, then Hilal Kordofan, named after the most famous football club in Sudan and the province where the Nuba Mountains are officially located. Each club is structured in the same way as other football clubs,[54] including having elected executive committees comprised of fifteen members, many of

[53] Beautiful artwork of sowing fine beads into bracelets, necklaces, and earrings.

[54] The analogy with football clubs is viable because there were many of them in the shantytowns at that time, participating in a youth league.

whom were former wrestlers or from old clan groups, beside some wealthy traders and educated people. There are eight clubs competing in the Wehda el Wataniya arena, who also form the local association of wrestling through regular elections, with this local association also being part of the national association of wrestling.[55] This association is part of the Olympic Committee of Sudan, which means that it can compete in different international sport events that include wrestling,[56] although the type of wrestling practiced in the shantytown is different from the standard Roman wrestling.

There are two types of arrangement to the competitions between the clubs. The first is club against club, where every club should bring a complete team of fifteen wrestlers. The wrestlers are arranged in three levels: the knights, the mediums, and the youths. Each match includes about twenty rounds or more, with rounds lasting for five minutes each; if there is no winner, the round is considered a draw. When the referee give the whistle for beginning the match, about six players from different levels should go out and wait beside the circled arena, then from the other side, any wrestler who would like to compete with one of those six would move up and give a sign of interest—usually in a dramatic way. The wrestler beside the arena has then the right to refuse by withdrawn himself towards his team bench. In fact the process of choosing the opponent is very intriguing, almost more than the fighting itself. Though, as a rule, it is not possible for a wrestler to challenge someone from a lower level, the opposite is possible, especially if a wrestler wants to promote himself to a higher level. Also if the wrestler is too strong, no one would challenge him, even if someone try his supporters will refuse; even his coach might refuse, and if that happens the wrestler cannot fight.

The second arrangement is what is called "national." In this, the teams divide into two camps. The southern side includes four clubs, and the northern side includes the other four. Every club brings one knight, two mediums, and three youths. Every wrestler dresses in his own club's t-shirt, and wrestlers move at the time of opponent's choice, where every club wrestlers move together. This type of arrangement is actually more

---

55 The national association of wrestling also includes associations from other states (e.g. Al-Jazeera, Blue Nile), but surprisingly there is no association in South Kordofan where the Nuba Mountains are located.

56 In fact members of the association are very proud that they participated in different wrestling events for the International Association of Wrestling or the International Olympic Committee in Turkey, South Korea, Senegal, and Qatar.

popular among the fans, because it usually brings the most popular wrestlers, unlike the club vs. club type, where sometimes the show might be very unequal, because there are significant differences in resources available to clubs.

For that reason, some clubs are able to attract the best wrestlers at any time. The financial rewards for the wrestlers depend largely upon their level, and their success within their level. The contract for a wrestler lasts for three years, including a minimum number of matches to play during the three seasons. The money is usually to be paid in installments: for a knight wrestler, the amount was between 3000-5000 SDG (about $860-1430), then in every match any player was to receive extra money (15 SDG/$4.50), with less than that for the training sessions. Usually the wrestlers depend upon what the fans give them after they beat their opponents, or even when they deliver an impressive performance. In that regard, the popularity of the wrestler to a large extent determines the quantity of reward he might receive, although popularity in many cases depends mainly on the quality of the performance that the wrestler is able to deliver. I remember one time when two wrestlers came to compete for the first time in the arena, starting in the youth level, but soon they beat all their opponents in this level. One day they tried to compete with every single player, but all refused to fight against them; then a wealthy man came out and showered them with money, amidst frenzied chanting from the supporters of the northern side. Someone told me Esaf (lit. Ambulance), the most popular knight, might collect about 2000 SDG ($570) in a good match.

The problem that the clubs encountered was how to secure enough money to pay the high cost of having good wrestlers. The main source of money for the clubs was the revenue of matches, with this revenue divided between the association (30%) to meet the administrative cost of running the show, and the rest divided between the two clubs, or the eight clubs if it is a national match. The average revenue of the club vs. club type of event was about 1500 SDG ($430), on a good day where the arena is full of fans. While the club on average includes thirty wrestlers (four knights, six mediums, and twenty youths), each month some of them needed to receive some amount of their contract fee, beside other expenses. That meant there was an inevitable deficit in the clubs' budgets, and they needed to depend upon other sources. Some clubs have wealthy members on the executive committees, or among elite fans, while other clubs oblige their members to pay on a regular basis and their executive committee members pay more to fill the gaps.

What makes wrestling a particularly interesting event to watch is the lively exchange between the actors involved in creating it, and, through this interplay between actors, the creation of wrestling's own rules and ceremonies. The rules of the game are ever changing, ready to be modified by the continually evolving surroundings of the show. For example, the referee is officially responsible for applying the rules of the game and determines who is winner in every round, but sometimes—if the referee delivers a poor judgment that the majority agreed was faulty—the fans might end the match in protest. In fact, the fans have a very strong influence in many respects; they might refuse a choice made by wrestler or his coach, largely because there is no barrier between the fans and the arena, although the police keep a persistent presence in the arena.

The rules of the game are very different to the rules in the original area; this is not always welcomed by the wrestlers who keep moving between the Nuba Mountains and Wehda el Wataniya arena. These changes are necessary to meet the standards of modern sport that the wrestling administrators are aspiring to achieve. For example, it is not possible to hit the opponent in his face, while that is one of the basic techniques of traditional wrestling in the Nuba Mountains. Also, it is not possible to hurt the opponent, and if any blood injury appears, the round should be stopped even if the wrestlers would like to continue; there is always medical assistance outside the arena to evaluate the situation. Besides this, many other ways of attacking and holding the opponent are not acceptable, while these are considered as an integral part of the home area wrestling tradition. The referee has also the right to give the player a warning about their misbehavior, and even dismiss them through a red card.

The match usually finished about half an hour before sunset. About one-third of the fans stay for some time to chat about what happened during the match, and to mock the fans from the other side. It seems like this part of exchange between the fans is no less important than the match itself. Some of the fans try to meet their champions and praise them, while association members and club administrators engage in endless meetings and discussion about the affairs of the wrestling. Small children set up their own arena and try to imitate their heroes, amidst strong encouragement from older people, who might try to teach the children some tricks of the fighting. Certainly, those older people try to create the wrestlers of tomorrow. These activities continue in the large tent until the area becomes dark and people start to disperse.

Recently the government built a new stadium to host the wrestling, in a nearby area just on the opposite side of the street, but still part of the large market.[57] By any standard, this a very surprising gesture from a government which is not willing to provide basic services to the shantytowns, like water and electricity, which are largely financed by people themselves. During my following of Nuba wrestling (lasting about four months), I witnessed a visit from the governor of Khartoum State and the governor of the locality. The governor of Khartoum State came to watch the final of the Sudan Championship of Wrestling, alongside many other ministers of Khartoum State; he came very late but managed to distribute prizes to the winners.[58] In fact, this is the only place where you can see officials in the shantytowns.[59] Thus for the government officials, the wrestling arena gives them a platform to meet shantytown people and gain their allegiance and support, or at least to show shantytown people that they consider them as a part of the capital city. This also gives the opportunity to local politicians to get access to promoting themselves; when the governor of Khartoum State came to the arena, the deputy of the wrestling association of Khartoum State gave a long speech praising the governor and leading the chanting of famous Islamic slogans of government supporters.[60]

Being a tourist destination is also another factor that encouraged the popularity of wrestling in the capital as a whole. It is not rare to see many foreigners come to watch the wrestling. Recently there was a popular journalistic story, "a barefoot Japanese diplomat wrestles for peace in Sudan"; the story describes Yasuhiro Murotatsu, a Japanese diplomat who engaged in wrestling about four times in the Wehda el Wataniya arena. Each time he goes, his story becomes more popular in the international media, and because of his story I was able to see many pictures of

[57] Until I finished the fieldwork it was still under construction (April 2012), but few months later it opened officially.

[58] The winner of the championship was the Khartoum State team, because it is by far the most advanced team compared with the other two teams (from Al-Jazeera and Blue Nile states).

[59] At least during my stay in the field; I encountered them in the wrestling arena and the opening ceremony of the football stadium.

[60] He is a young lawyer, seemingly interested in the privilege of the position more than the wrestling, as I rarely saw him in the arena for watching the matches.

the new stadium.[61] This constant popularity of wrestling attracts the local media to increasingly cover its events. A few years ago, the Association of Nuba Wrestling changed its name to the Association of Sudanese Wrestling: on the one hand, because the association sought more recognition and participation internationally, and on the other because the association sought to portray itself as representing the whole country, and the whole capital city by extension. Therefore, through these delicate processes of localization, Nuba wrestling started as tribal fighting and as an amateur sport engaged in by people only drawn from the Nuba Mountains. Currently, however, it has evolved to be not only the most popular sport in the shantytowns, but also a national sport representing the whole country.

Figure 12: Photo of Nuba Wrestling 1

Wrestling matches take place three times weekly, with the largest on Fridays. El-Wehda, fieldwork 2012.

[61] I saw the story covered in many international news outlets, such as BBC, Al-Jazeera, and Sudanese news websites. For example:
http://www.bbc.com/news/world-africa-24960219,
http://www.japantimes.co.jp/news/2013/09/06/national/diplomat-wrestles-for-peace-in-riven-sudan/#.VClFhtIW2ek.

Figure 13: Photo of Nuba Wrestling 2

Children trying to imitate what they have seen in the arena, after the match, fieldwork 2012.

7.3 Auto-Rickshaw Drivers

After the planning of Al-Baraka in 1994, many paved roads started to cross the area, during which time the numbers of auto-rickshaws increased in different parts of Khartoum as a means of transportation for short distances inside different neighborhoods. Until that time, people had used donkey carts to reach the large market from inside Al-Baraka. Gradually, more rickshaws dominated the scene, until it became the only means of local transportation: rickshaws are faster and the fare price was the same, and it takes less time to start each journey compared with the donkey carts, which need far more people to be full and start travelling. In the beginning, the owners of the rickshaws were from outside the shantytowns, although the drivers were mostly from among the second generation youths.

Young people in Al-Baraka have strong relationships with technology, although they are mostly dropouts from schools, particularly from primary level. Since childhood, these young people are obsessed with PlayStations, whereby in every street there is one or more shop for group playing. Subsequently, mobile phones have also occupied an increasingly prominent place in daily activities and conversations between young people.[62] The presence of satellite TVs has also become one of the most important mediums for communicating with the global world. The presence of satellite TVs takes two forms: firstly, in homes, where nearly every house connected with electricity has a satellite TV;[63] even if some houses lack this facility, it is very usual to share watching satellite TV with immediate neighbors, and is one common way to strengthen social relations. In many cases, neighbors actually live in one house, as many houses host more than one family.[64] The second form is watching satellite TV in viewing clubs, which are spread all over Al-Baraka, even in the neighborhoods but mostly in the service area. This type mostly targets male youth, with most programs focused on movies, sport, and music.

The most advanced connection with technology comes with rickshaw motors, through the wide spread of rickshaws in the neighborhoods, in the homes of the owners or the drivers. The rickshaws have become part of daily life experiences of people, especially younger people. In this sense, learning how to drive a rickshaw is a part of the normal skills that young people try to acquire.[65] While the younger generation shares the knowledge and practice of rickshaw technology, other social groups like the first generation and the educated have become increasingly excluded from this experience, and by extension excluded from connection with this form of global knowledge. Certainly, the monopoly of this global knowledge gives the youth a particular power and influence: so the attitude of welcoming and venturing into every new opportunity becomes an integral part of youths' self-conceptions. Across the entire African continent, it is not just the participation, appropriation and practices of youth in social, religious and political institutions that highlights their centrality in contemporary affairs, but also their localization of technological and

---

[62] Although at the time of fieldwork (2010-2012) smart phones were not popular, because they were so expensive, still many varieties of Nokia and Samsung mobile phones were subject to competition between young people.

[63] I noticed, from the houses I managed to visit in the field, having satellite TV seems a higher priority than many other electric appliances such as a refrigerator, tape recorder, and oven.

[64] Renting part of the house is a common practice to increase the income of older settlers, also because one room and a small verandah in front of it is considered a sufficient space to rent and live in.

[65] Interestingly in the big market there is place where youngsters can hire motorbikes or cars and drive for short distances around the market, but there is no section for rickshaw hiring.

discursive innovations. Globally, youth are especially venturing into new techniques of practicing, earning and communicating as ways of gaining life chances (Christiansen et al. 2006: 20).

A rickshaw is a simple three-wheeled vehicle with a very simple design and engine, although with a two-stroke engine fueled by benzene mixed with car oil, it is very polluting, and the engine needs to be cleaned every week or ten days. Usually, this happens in the neighborhood, specifically in the stations (the local name of the place where young people hang out during the day). In the station, you can usually find younger youths who are still in their school years sitting around. They are willing to help the drivers in the process of cleaning the engine, which includes dismantling the interior of the rickshaw, through which younger youth gradually learn the mechanics of the rickshaw; indeed, some of them might exceed the knowledge of the drivers: "but the fact remains that reopening a stable technology at the user level—modding—rests on a foundation of conditions, mainly skills and creativity, which are still largely unaccounted for" (Beck 2009: 155). After finishing the cleaning of the engine, they will all go to a nearby water channel to wash themselves and the body of the rickshaw. In the distance between Al-Baraka and the channel, those youths might have their first opportunity to drive a rickshaw, whereby the younger generation start on their way to becoming drivers, usually after they drop out of schooling (see Figure No. 15).

Owning a rickshaw is a very lucrative business, whereby daily net earnings might reach SDG70-100 ($20-28). This makes it far more lucrative than the normal salary of formal employment,[66] and one of the best paid compared with other informal (self-employed) jobs. In the case of hiring a driver, there are two ways to divide the earnings, the first of which involves sharing the income equally between the driver and the owner after cutting the costs of running the rickshaw.[67] In this case, there would be mutual trust between the two parties, because there is no way to check the actual earning of the rickshaw. The second type is by stating a permanent rate of money to the owner, which usually depends upon the

---

[66] Formal jobs in governmental institutions start from about SDG700 ($200) monthly for graduates, and far less for lower qualifications, where the majority of shantytown people might find formal jobs.

[67] The cost of running a rickshaw is usually very low because it consumes about 82 miles to the gallon; in addition to car oil, the average driver pays SDG12 for benzene and SDG4 for oil daily, and spare parts are all imported from India.

condition of the rickshaw. The very new and well-equipped rickshaws allow the owner to expect SDG40 ($11) per day, and less equipped rickshaws generate at least SDG20 ($5.50) for the owner, with the remainder going to the driver after cutting the running costs. This way is preferable for the owners, but it has the danger of subjecting the rickshaw to overwork, which lead to a short life span. This is the case because many drivers hire another driver (secretly) to work during his rest time, locally called a jockey, thus enabling the driver to maximize his share. This actually leads to tension and mistrust in the relationship between owners and drivers, as well as accusations of exploitation between the two parties, especially because the cost of maintenance for larger mechanical problems is the responsibility of the owner.

In the early days following the introduction of rickshaws in the shantytowns, the owners tended to be from outside the shantytowns or traders and educated people from the shantytowns. Soon, the drivers realized the potential for profitability, and started to use the method of revolving saving money (locally called a saving box), whereby ten to fifteen drivers each collect about SDG25 ($7) per day, and every four to six months one of them uses the money to buy a new rickshaw (about SDG 17,500 or $5,000). In this way, many drivers in Al-Baraka own their own rickshaws; for instance, my immediate neighbors on my first field trip, two brothers aged under thirty, each had two rickshaws, while another person in the neighborhood owned four rickshaws. The ownership of their rickshaws made the drivers rich and powerful, allowing them to redefine themselves and introduce themselves as more respected and hardworking youths.

Driving a rickshaw is always considered a very risky profession; indeed, my immediate neighbor (who owned two rickshaws) had an accident while he was driving, when a saloon car hit his rickshaw from behind in a congested turn; he was carrying a woman, the rickshaw and turned upside down three times. Luckily, he only suffered minor injuries to his legs and back, while the woman injured her face. In the same week, another accident happened in the shantytown, when a priest was hit by a speeding rickshaw while he was riding his bicycle on the street, dying in the hospital a few days later. The accident was very widely publicized, and I even read about it in the Juba Post newspaper[68].

In fact, some rickshaw drivers are very careless and immature, as many of them are still teenagers, and they do not have driving licenses.

[68] The Juba Post, Vol. 6 Issue 65, 2-5 August 2010: 12.

On many occasions, I saw them driving very dangerously on the street, and when there were no other vehicles, they might show off their abilities by driving two rickshaws together in line, with each driver trying to put his foot on the other rickshaw in a very dangerous manner, because the paved roads are narrow and there is no barrier between the two opposite directions.

One day there were many youth in the station, including a rickshaw driver, and we were talking about rickshaw accidents. Many of them blamed irresponsible drivers, and especially car drivers, because they usually have full car insurance and thus do not care about smaller vehicles such as rickshaws, because they know it has no ability to harm their cars. Some of the attendants also blamed the rickshaw drivers for racing against each other to reach passengers, especially in the morning when people come out from their houses. At this point, the rickshaw driver felt that they were pointing at him, so he started to defend himself. He insisted that drivers are not bad people who want to harm others, but rather the nature of a profession like this, if a rickshaw driver wants to be successful he should be fast and able to race and compete with other drivers, otherwise he would not be able to survive among them. He stated that the slogan of rickshaw drivers is that "*your money is in your accelerator*", which for him means that the more you increase your speed and skills, the more money you can earn and become successful. When others showed their disapproval, he maintained that life and death is just a destiny. Besides, accidents leading to injuries and deaths of people happen everywhere and all the time, and he considers it as a part of the job.

A few days later, I was taking a rickshaw towards the large market, when I noticed that the rickshaw was moving very slowly and others were passing us easily. As the driver was an old man and his rickshaw was a little old, I was not surprised. I then realized that the journey is very boring, and you feel as if you are walking, because the distance is about eight kilometers and the rickshaw itself is not a very fast vehicle.[69] Moreover, the rickshaw lacked audio music streaming. For this reason, it seems that speedier rickshaws run by youth and supplied with strong sound systems are very attractive for many passengers, even if they are more dangerous. Actually, this is what usually happened in the large

---

[69] One driver told me the maximum speed in the speedometer is 80km, but actually reaching this speed might cause the rickshaw to turn upside down, because it is very light. Practically, the maximum speed is 65km, with four passengers in it.

market, because you find many rickshaws waiting for passengers, who make their choice according to the above-mentioned criteria.

Figure 14: Photo of Rickshaw Drivers 1

Rickshaws dominated the streets of shantytowns even in the main market. El-Wehda market, fieldwork 2012.

Figure 15: Photo of Rickshaw Drivers 2

Young people sitting in the neighborhood, while some help in rickshaw cleaning. Al-Baraka, fieldwork 2011.

7.4 Private Schools

Since 1991, it is possible to open private schools in the country as a part of the economic liberalization policy adopted by the government (Bakhit 1994: 254). Private schools usually offer higher quality education, albeit while charging expensive fees.[70] The idea found its way to Al-Baraka shantytown before the policy, through small centers for educating adult students, besides illiteracy education for older people, and these centers subsequently switched their activities towards teaching children. After a few years, some graduates who were teaching in those centers started their own private schools, which soon became very successful, prompting more private schools to open their doors. In the 2010-2011 school year, there were 3802 pupils attending private schools,[71] while there were 2264 pupils attending public schools, meaning that private schools in Al-Baraka enrolled 62.7% of the total primary schools pupils (see Figures Nos. 16 and 17). Indeed, one public school closed its doors because there were not enough children.

[70] There are huge variations between the fees of private primary schools in Khartoum: For wealthy families it costs about 40,000 SDG ($16,607) per year for international schools (which offer British and American curricula) (Pantuliano 2011: 26-27). For middle class people it costs about SDG 1,000 ($413), while for shantytown people it costs between SDG 135-200 ($53-82) per year.

[71] The number might be higher because there were many informal schools, which taught pupils until seventh grade then moved them to formal schools to sit for the final primary school examination.

Figure 16: Number of Pupils in Private Primary Schools in Al-Baraka, 2010-2011 School Year

Name	First class		Second class		Third class		Fourth-class		Fifth class		Sixth class		Seventh class		Eighth class		Total		
	boys	girls	boys	girls	boys	girls	boys	girls	boys	girls	boys	girls	boys	girls	boys	girls	boys	girls	total
Al-Shakrin	36	73	53	49	55	51	50	50	19	31	35	34	44	39	34	42	326	369	695
Al-Hegazi	27	32	19	19	23	19	19	19	14	16	16	15	11	23	16	15	145	158	303
Al-Barakat	70	45	76	41	67	40	83	23	62	31	70	38	63	44	50	25	541	287	828
Al-Afrah	12	4	12	6	10	5	4	19	4	7	8	7	9	6	18	6	77	60	137
Al-Mohandis	36	34	36	48	36	47	46	45	42	39	29	36	28	39	30	33	283	321	604
Al-Imam Muslim	25	15	28	10	26	10	20	15	30	12	25	19	12	10	48	50	214	141	355
Al-Doha	34	41	44	36	44	36	51	36	36	37	34	47	37	36	24	39	304	308	612
Al-Rahma	24	24	20	16	17	25	16	10	18	23	14	7	13	9	18	14	140	128	268
total																	**2030**	**1772**	**3802**

Source: The Office of Education, El-Haj Yousif Administrative Unit, East Nile Locality.

Figure 17: Number of Pupils in Public Primary Schools in Al-Baraka, 2010-2011 School Year

Name	No. of pupils	No. of teachers
Bilal Ibn Rabah Boys	**236**	**14**
Abu-Bakr Al-Siddig Boys	**428**	**13**
Arrok Ton Boys	**199**	**12**
Al-Megdad Ibn Al-Asod Boys	**279**	**12**
Al-Salam Girls	**228**	**12**
Isfya Badr Girls	**327**	**11**
Al-Tadmon Al-Shabby Girls	**210**	**13**
Imena Bint Wahab Girls	**357**	**11**
total	**2264**	**98**

Source: The Office of Primary Education, East Nile Locality.

Those private schools became more successful in Al-Baraka despite being more expensive, where parents have to pay about SDG15 ($4.30) per child per month, and the majority of parents have more than one child attending schools, as in the case of Magada Adam.

> "I get the expenditure of the home daily, my husband work[s] by a daily wage, how I can get it monthly? He gives me about 10-12 pounds, it is not enough but I try to manage, how do you find something enough in this Sudan? …. The expenditure of the schools are monthly, the three kids in the school need 45 pound every one 15, the one who in kindergarten needs 30 pounds in a month, for the breakfast I give them 3.70 pounds, 0.70 pound[s] for the kindergarten and the three pounds for the rest …. I am working in the market, I sell vegetables in the ground (*farsha*), I worked since 3-4 years ago, it was first time for me to work…. My aunts and sister who work there told me about that and help me until I could learn it…. I do not earn something fixed, the market is the prophet bowl, one day like that, and other day like this… what I earn sometimes enough for me, and sometimes not enough, the day that the market is good, one can do what she

> want, but if the day is bad, you should be patient until tomorrow may be better… I save some money by participate in box (revolving money), but when I take the money, give some to this person, and some to others, and the kids, and the rent, and the work of our father (husband) the today's livelihood, it is not enough."

The reasons for preferring private schools is that they are usually able to achieve better results in the final primary school examination, even though private schools have less resources and spaces (as they are usually run in small houses) and the teachers are normally not trained to teach in primary schools. However, because those graduates are educated people from the area, they have a strong motivation to serve the children, and they look on what they are doing as a noble cause; it also helps them to generate valuable income, especially for the school owners, as well as giving them more social standing and power in the area.

Extra lessons are usually offered in the afternoon in private schools. Monthly examinations are imposed upon pupils, and they maintain regular contact with the parents, informing them about the performance of their children, as well as their attendance. Furthermore, for the seventh and eighth classes, the school keeps them in the classrooms until early evening to revise their lessons. Through such measures, private schools are not only replacing public schools, but adding new dimensions to the role that schools play in the Al-Baraka community, creating a space for interaction between different educated people's generations, and helping educated people to assert themselves and organize their actions to gain more power and influence in the area.

The main difference between the private and public schools relates to the teaching methods used in the two different categories. In public schools, the teachers are mostly from outside the shantytowns, and they consider their presence in the area as punishment from their bosses, because according to the bureaucratic hierarchy in education and other services, institutions located in shantytowns offer lower status and rewards than those in wealthier and middle class parts of the city. Thus, teachers in public schools are reluctant to deliver their best, and also do not fully understand how the community and socio-cultural environment affects their pupils, so they are less able to understand the specific variations of the shantytowns. Accordingly, their methods of teaching and delivering the school curriculum are likely to be ineffective. On the other hand, the owners and teachers of private schools are from the community, and received their education from other parts of the city, thus enabling them to understand the variations and the obstacles facing their pupils. Indeed, Kaltom Adam's career demonstrates this:

> "I am [a] teacher in El-Rahma private school, I started as teacher since 1996, but I started here in El-Rahma school since 2000, before that I was teaching in Abu-Baker El-Siddig public school, I worked also with the charity and voluntary organizations and the popular committee, also I worked in the communal work (*estinfar*) of Zad-alkhier, I worked also in basic relief courses two times, also I worked in connecting the water in the area, also I worked as representative of women in the popular committee, and currently I work as teacher in the school, I started the public work since 1990, I started this work because of my efforts and relations in the neighborhood, when some work come to people they nominate me to do it, then I go and do it, my husband and the people of the neighborhood encourage me and help me, while I like teaching from my young age, I was going to charity organization in some days or weekly, and the basic relief course I was going daily until I received the certificate from the ministry of health, and the teaching of course in permanent character, except in the formal holidays, my salary is 375 pounds, I use it to help my brothers and my family only, and sometimes I pay for the charity organization as charity (*sadaga*), I choose this job, because it is honor job, and it is good job even it has reward from God (*agur*), also it is humanitarian job, I always like two professions: the medical, and teaching.... I didn't face problems with my family or with men or with the government at any time."

I visited the most successful private schools in the areas, and interviewed their headmasters, besides visiting three other public schools. The difference in understanding the right methods to deliver the curriculum to the pupils is obvious. In Al-Barkat private school, there are 828 pupils, while most crowded public schools enroll half these numbers, at 428 pupils. In Al-Doha primary school, the rate of success in the 2010-2011 primary examination was 100%, whereby all 52 pupils passed, with the lowest degree being 175 and the best scoring 260, while 38 pupils scored above 200 out of 280. Three private schools achieved a 100% rate that year, based upon which the East Nile locality ranked third in whole Khartoum State, exceeding the central locality.[72]

---

[72] There are seven localities in Khartoum state; three located in centers of the three towns comprised Khartoum, usually those three central localities ranking better in all sorts of services delivered to the population.

In the successful private schools, there are very strict measures to control the pupils, primarily focused on attendance, because the majority of pupils come from poor uneducated families. There is usually no pressure from the parents towards their children to be in the school every day or complete their homework in the evenings, which is thus left for the teachers to ensure. Although the measures of controlling the pupils tend to depend upon physical punishment as a basic means, other methods of punishment, like forcing the pupils to do extra homework or solitary confinement for a few hours, are sometimes used. There are also measures to increase the subject knowledge of pupils, especially in the last year before the examinations. Besides staying for longer hours in schools, there are different methods of revising lessons; in Al-Doha school, the first method is individual reading, and subsequently if the results are not as expected then they try with group revision, before finally switching to revising with a teacher.

In Al-Barakat private school, each pupil should have a guardian responsible for taking care of him or her, paying the fees and being in contact with the school. Without this, enrollment is not possible, while in the case of public schools or even some private schools this is not always the case. Even sometimes, the parents might change the school of their child many times during the year if they wish, usually based upon the complaints of their child. In Al-Doha school, there are some teachers who are very famous as good and funny teachers in whole of Al-Baraka; they are also the only private school that pays attention to non-academic activities for the pupils, organizing groups for music, sports, and theatre. Furthermore, every year they organize a large celebration for the graduates. These different methods have allowed private schools to attract more pupils and achieve more success compared to the public schools.

Officially, those private schools are categorized as "schools of special conditions" by the office of primary education in the Haj Yousif Administrative Unit, to which the Al-Baraka area administratively belongs.[73] This is a designation meant to differentiate them from other primary private schools in other parts of the locality, where the requirements to open a private school are more expensive. For example, a primary private school in a middle class area should have at least 1000m^2 size and classrooms with ventilation facilities, all teachers should be graduates from universities, and the new schools need to pay SDG10,000

[73] Interview with the head of primary private schools in El-Haj Yousif Administrative Unit, 15 July 2010.

($2875) as fees of registration in the office. For "schools of special conditions," the requirements are not very strict, in the sense that there is no need to meet all of the above-mentioned criteria, apart from paying SDG1000 ($275), even in installments, to be registered with the office. However, registration does not offer the private schools in Al-Baraka any tangible difference, aside from being officially recognized and attending monthly meeting for headmasters in the Office, and the schools becoming able to examine their pupils in the final primary level examinations. Compared with public schools, the Office of Education in the locality is more out of touch with "schools of special conditions." There are very rare visits from the Office to monitor and offer advice on the situations of those schools, which has prompted many informal schools to run in the neighborhoods. It might be obvious here that the two types of primary private schools in the categorization of the official governmental circles is just a reflection of how the urban government divides the city. The official explanation for differentiating the "schools of special conditions" is that because the people living there are poorer and affected by war and drought in their original areas, relaxing the bureaucratic measures of opening private schools would enable the population to afford good education at a good price. However, the question remains concerning whether this is the only way to offer good education to the shantytown's population, because the main task of local government is ideally to deliver education through public schools. This means that any efforts to help the shantytown's "special needs" should start from the direct services offered by the government itself, in the case of education through public rather than private schools.

The naming of private schools compared with the public schools is also an important indicator of the relationship between the shantytowns and the rest of the city. Most of the public schools' names originate from Islamic history (four names of the prophet's companions, and one for all companions together), while in primary private schools one is named for an Islamic scholar. Indeed, because the government is adopting urban Islam as its main ideology and trying to impose it upon the entire population, it is unsurprising that schools are named this way. However, owners and teachers choose the names of their private schools in a different way: for example Al-Barakat from Al-Baraka (singular), Al-Mohandis, meaning an engineer, Al-Rahma, Al-Afrah, and Al-Shakrin which all mean "good deeds." This clearly shows a different way to define themselves, and that the ideology imposed upon them through the bureaucratic measures and institutions is not convincing and does not work. In this way, naming the primary private schools differently, and using different methods to teach pupils, are all concerted efforts to establish a different identity for the shantytowns.

Another important issue is the school curriculum, which is designed and produced by the Ministry of Education through the Administration of Curricula and Educational Research. Almost all teachers, even in public schools, agree about the problems of the new curriculum imposed two decades ago. They criticize many aspects of it, starting from the heavy load placed upon the children, and what is called the "comprehensive curriculum", which starts by teaching the children writing and sentences, before learning letters and word constructions. This new method proved unsuccessful in the private schools in Al-Baraka, and now all of them teach the children in the initial classes with the old system, simply because the current curriculum system was designed for children who attended pre-school for two years before starting primary school, which is not the case all the time.

Moreover, there is a problem of language and the subjects of the curriculum, which have all been constructed in a way that is appropriate for the middle class of northern origin. In shantytowns, Arabic it is not always the language of the families, and even the spoken language on the street of shantytowns is a variant on Sudanese urban Arabic. Furthermore, the material lives of children lack many aspects and issues introduced in the curriculum. Generally, what is lacking in the curriculum seems to be any acknowledgement of the diversity of the people living in Sudan and in the capital, in the sense that the curricula only reflects one worldview and ideology, representing the powerful groups who are controlling the bureaucratic machine that produces these curricula.

7.5 The Localization Process

From these three examples, it is now possible to ascertain the main characteristics of the localization process concept. Initially, the localization typically starts with some pioneers who introduce ideas from three sources (i.e. the homeland, middle class areas, and globalized youth culture). Subsequently, an idea might be taken up by others who are able to make more modifications, which usually makes it more acceptable, before passing through constant negotiations between what came from outside in the beginning, and what sorts of changes and modifications can be added to make it more appropriate and fulfilling for local needs. This process continues until the ideas reach a point whereby they are considered part of the local community, and until no one attributes it to its original sources. This movement usually starts from one corner of the triangle, within which the pioneers are situated (see Figure No. 18), before gradually moving towards the center of the triangle. Indeed, the more it moves inside, the more the processes of localization can be considered successful, ending in the point of full localization, usually with a different name and a history only traceable to the local pioneers.

From this, we can identify four criteria for localization processes to become fully completed. Firstly, when the imported idea is re-named locally, as in the case of Nuba wrestling, which people usually refer to simply as wrestling and which is officially called Sudanese wrestling. In the case of rickshaws and private schools, these still maintain their original names, although the pronunciations and connotations are very much local. Secondly is the flexibility and regular modifications to the innovation, through which many new and different details are added, such as the incorporation of football rules in wrestling, or in adding extra devices to the rickshaws to increase the volume of noise coming out of the exhaust pipe, and adding a sound system to allow local rap music to play and to be heard widely. Thirdly is creating a system of knowledge transmission and training to younger generations, through which the new localized idea is guaranteed to continue and become renewable; for example, the imitation of wrestling by children after every match, the presence of youngsters in the station during the cleaning of the rickshaws, or the dream of many pupils to become teachers when they graduate. Finally, the history of the localized idea usually only becomes traceable to the local pioneers, because the idea is perceived as coming from within the community, and if there is a suggestion of a connection with the original sources, this is usually ignored or deemed unimportant. This is evident in the case of wrestling, which popularly traced only to Hamed Elnil in Omdurman, or private schools traced by teachers to the centers of adult education.

Although localization process entail the idea that people are able to reproduce and re-invent what is coming from outside their communities, we still need to acknowledge the universal character of these processes: "the paradox that people in different world areas increasingly share aspirations, material standards, and social institutions at the same time that their local definition of and engagement with these initiatives fuels cultural distinctiveness" (Geschiere et al. 2008: 2). This facilitates communications between the local community and 'others,' in the sense that it becomes a simultaneous process of local-global. Certainly, these dynamics constantly evolve and function at different levels at the same time, which means everybody has the ability to take part; in fact, only through the participation of significant numbers of local community members can any process claim success. All this allows me to argue that meaningful social change only takes place in the local community through the localization process paradigm that I have outlined here (see Figure 19).

Figure 18: Diagram of the Localization Process

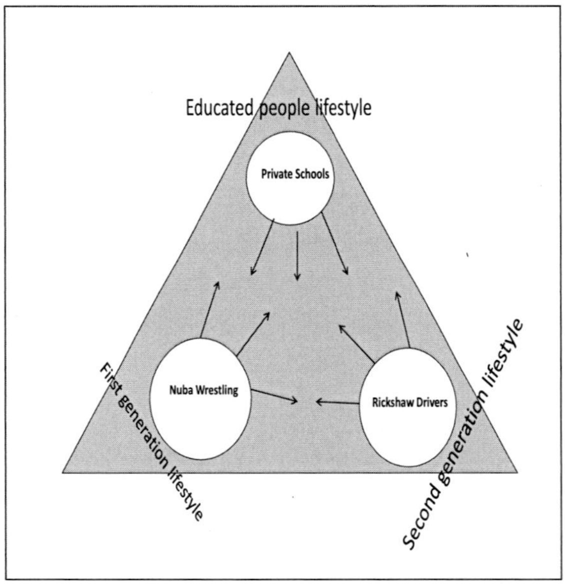

Chapter Eight: Construction and Re-construction of Identity and Lifestyles

8.1 Introduction

One of the crucial questions this thesis has tried to answer is: what happens when a community of impoverished rural migrants from ethnic/religious minorities settles in a self-built shantytown? Moreover, what exactly happens when they are exposed to persistent pressure from the dominant urban middle class to be assimilated, and what are their alternatives? Do they tend to follow in the footsteps of their neighboring middle class areas, or might they resist by maintaining their culture and homeland identity, or try to find another new constructed lifestyle and identity—and if so, how do they manage to invent and create it?

The answer might be that neither of the two extreme options presented in these questions reflect the reality nor the direction of social change that takes place in the shantytowns in Khartoum and even elsewhere. Nonetheless, many features of the lifestyles of shantytowns resemble those of the city or home areas; still many other features are new and invented, just because these seem more appropriate and suitable to the conditions of the new residents. Indeed, because opting for only one distinct lifestyle is not an ideal option for the majority of the population, people tend to combine the three lifestyles at the same time, which is exactly what makes them distinctive from their urban neighbors, nor with their home area ancestors and relatives.

It might be clear by now that due to the enormous and diverse amount of challenges facing the shantytowns residents, they tend to form different social groups to express their different responses and the different experiences that they have acquired. These lifestyle groups of the first generation, the educated people, and the second generation, are the product of the conditions and circumstances of the complex reality of the shantytowns, which extends between the homeland and the capital. Moreover, this is exactly what makes the shantytowns a very distinctive entity, part of the city, yet a special part of it.

Thus, one of the important research findings here shows that when a community migrates or is displaced towards another (more "modern") area,[74] the host community usually expects an assimilatory attitude from the migrants. However, the result of these interactions is a newly constructed social identity that belongs to neither the homeland nor the host community. Moreover, it seems that the more time goes on, and the more generations who are born in the new community (shantytowns), the more this new distinctive identity and lifestyle will take shape and materiality, to the point that, in the future, no one will be able to describe it as different or alien, whether in the host community (the capital) or anywhere else.

8.2 Lessons from the Global South Urban Experience

It seems that there is an inevitable link between urban growth and slum expansion, not only in the global South, as we have been experiencing, but even more obviously in nineteenth century western Europe urbanization: although the European experience suggests that there were linkages between the prevalence of slums, and mass migration of rural workers seeking jobs in the growing industrialized economies. When we compare the Western urban experience with the recent explosion of slum dwellers in the Third World, it is easy to conclude that the linkage is simply between mass migration and urban expansion, whatever the reasons behind such mass migration.

The first experiences of slum sprawl occurred in nineteenth century Western Europe, largely attributed to industrialization. Meanwhile, the recent Third World experience of illegal squatting has been attributed to diverse push and pull factors, which drove the rural migrants out of their farms and attracted them to the peripheries of the city as their new settlement, although significant numbers of them are still pulled by industrial growth in large cities (e.g. across Asia). Even though there are many instances of forced migration owing to natural or man-made disasters, the destination of the affected population is usually an urban settlement, as opposed to a rural environment similar to their original lands.

From the two experiences of mass migration of poor rural people to the peripheries of large cities—with one and half century between

[74] Modernity here is very much relative and contextual, far from the simple uni-linear model of moving from the traditional (African) position toward the modern (Western). Because "the clarity promised by defining modernity is illusory. Rather than seeking to capture essential features of modernity in a universal frame, we propose to investigate modernity as a historical phenomenon that is still evolving, and to take into account the contradictions and ambivalences to which it give rise" (Geschiere et al. 2008: 2).

them—the same conditions of life are replicated to a surprising degree, including poor infrastructure and housing, and a lack of basic services. Even being highly dependent on the informal sector is typical, to the extent that we can imagine that walking in the poor areas of London in 1850s has a similar feel to roaming the back streets of Kolkata or Lagos today. This clearly further suggests that the current slum growth in the Third World is a direct product of the urbanization expansion taking place in the global South. Accordingly, if we want to study the phenomena of slums and shantytowns in the global South, the starting point should be urban growth, including its causes and dynamics.

Not only is it a vital question whether any rapid mass urbanization is necessarily accompanied by some sort of growth of poor settlements—as clearly evident—but also whether this always emerges with a specific type of urbanization (e.g. industrialization, informal urbanization, or colonial urbanization). Perhaps this question opens the door for a more accurate account of urban experiences in human history.

Some might argue that the prevalence of impoverished slums and shantytowns in the global South or even in nineteenth century western Europe and North America is and was a result of poverty, whereby the inhabitants were unable to afford basic needs, caused by their lack of skills enabling them to compete in capitalist urban economies. If we apply measurements of urban poverty (e.g. a lack of services, low incomes) to rural areas, we will certainly find that more poor people live in the countryside than in poor slums, which suggests that poverty is not a unique urban phenomenon, and even might be more acute in rural areas. In fact, the expectation of better and safer lives in slum areas is one of the strongest motives for moving from rural areas, as my case study has clearly showed. This might suggest that the kind of poverty and despair usually portrayed in the poor parts of the cities in the global South today—by different middle class outsiders—is perceived by its inhabitants as being a much better quality of life compared with life in their original areas, or at least more secure from natural and man-made disasters, which usually plagued rural home areas.

The fast growth of urban settlements in the last half of the twentieth century in global South countries exceeded any expectations of reports from international NGOs;[75] the same trend is notable in the statistics of

[75] UN Habitat estimated that, in 2008, half of the world's population lived in urban settlements, and in 2050 this was projected to rise to 70% of the world's population. The bulk of this urban population will be in developing regions, as the annual rate of urban

slum and shantytown populations, populating the peripheries of the same Third World cities. In ways that suggest the urban experiences of the global South are not only confined to the most poor rural migrants, this also includes all other segments of the population, and especially the growing numbers of newly-established middle classes, as we have clearly seen in the experiences of the emerging economies. In fact, the largest-scale urban structures are currently emerging in East Asia. The Pearl River (Hong Kong-Guangzhou) and the Yangze River (Shanghai) deltas, combined with the Beijing-Tianjin corridor, are on their way to becoming urban-industrial megalopolises comparable to previous capitalist corridors (e.g. Tokyo-Osaka, the lower Rhine, or New York-Philadelphia). According to two leading researchers, these new Chinese megalopolises are in the first stage of the emergence as 'a continuous urban corridor stretching from Japan/ North Korea to West Java' (Davis 2006: 7). As is predicted over the current century, this great dragon-like expansion of urban centers will constitute the material and demographic culmination of millennia of urban transformation (Davis 2006: 7). With this in mind, it is more realistic to look at slums and shantytowns expansion in the global South as an integral part of a huge transformation that is likely to affect the whole global South community, driven by mass industrialization (e.g. South East Asia, Latin America) and by the mass informality (e.g. Africa).

Poor urban people are still the most deprived sections of the population, although they are able to use their agency and power to make significant gains in their power relations with other parts of the city. I argue that this study has showed in detail how these power contests manifest themselves in complex layers. This includes a level between the slums and shantytowns against the rest of the urban classes, and on another subtle level, contestations also manifest themselves within the community of the shantytowns and slums.

8.3 Ethnicity as an Urban Phenomenon

As stated in the introduction of this thesis, I proposed that the concept of ethnicity is not suitable for understanding and analyzing the shantytown communities in Khartoum, given that many differences still exist be-

growth in those regions is 2.27%, while only 0.47% in developed regions (UN Habitat 2009: 8).

tween different social groups that cannot be explained without using other sets of categorization, based upon the lifestyles as a main criteria.

Nonetheless, it is still important to tackle the subject of ethnic groups thoroughly for two reasons: firstly, for practical reasons, since ethnicity played a very important role in the past, especially during the time of the areas' formation. Furthermore, ethnic groups are still playing a significant role in the first generation's perception of life. This can be noticed from their activities and daily social life, which are inclined towards keeping the traditions of the home areas before their migration as much as possible. However, we have to be very careful about making generalizations about the first generation, as there are many apparent differences between economic migrants and forced migrants.

Secondly, for theoretical reasons, ethnicity is still a new field of study in social sciences, given that it only appeared in the 1960s. Nevertheless, it proved its importance to studying various issues, with many scholars considering it part of history, including issues such as tribalism, myths of origins, shared languages and religions in the modern states. As increasing conflicts arise in the world along the lines of ethnic divisions, the issue of identity politics has become central to many studies in different social disciplines. At the societal level, many scholars and politicians have taken the nation-state as the main representative of people, and on the level of communities they considered the class and gender as main categories that divide people. However, later on the experience of the newly established nations endured many problems due to the existence of other criteria that still divide the people everywhere in the world (e.g. ethnicity).

This suggests that ethnicity remains a vital tool to analyze and understand urban experiences. It is important not only as an analytical tool to categorize different segments of the urban population, but also to enable differentiation and comparisons between them. The problem of ethnicity lies in its inability to catch up with the rapid changes that always occur in multi-ethnic urban spaces. Accordingly, ethnicity suffers from being a static concept, only dealing with the past of the ever-changing reality of human beings living in a constantly shifting environment. This critique, as I have shown in the empirical account of this study, suggests that there is a need to find another concept or set of concepts to allow us to capture the reality of shantytown communities. This new conception must reveal the subtle realities and everyday practices of the communities. What is needed is a concept that can reflect a category of analysis and a category of practice, in the sense that we can use it to describe and analyze everyday practices empirically, as well as using it in abstract ways in our academic theorizations and comparisons.

8.4 Ethnic Identity, or rather Social Identity

Even with the recent major consensus in ethnicity studies based upon the viability of constructivism and instrumentalism as mainstream approaches, there remains a lack of consistency in using the concept of ethnic identity. This concept, with its recent extension to the idea of ethnic politics, involves a wide-ranging popularity in many different social studies, as it explains many aspects of recent high profile ethnic conflicts in the world, in addition to the rise of ethnic sentiments within nations; many scholars assumed wrongly that the formation of the nation state would force local communities to discard their ethnic bonds and substitute it with nationalistic sentiments. The dream was of a melting pot filled with different ethnic groups, and with the use of the nation state as a main vehicle or the pot itself, all different groups would emerge eventually as one group, under one flag and national anthem. Those scholars and politicians realized their misjudgment through the persistence of ethnic conflicts and divides, even in Europe, where the classical nation state had emerged. They found in the concept of identity politics an ultimate solution to their dilemma about the causes of the revival of ethnic sentiments (Brubaker and Cooper 2000: 1).

Nevertheless, many loopholes exist in the concept of ethnic identity that need to be addressed. Firstly, the concept is still focused on the cultural aspects of the life of communities, even within the constructivism-instrumentalist approach, and particularly the use of shared history, whereby the origins, same language and region are seen as the main characteristics of ethnic groups. Indeed, those aspects are the exact subject of revival by political movements, whether it is called nationalistic or ethnic nationalism. This might suggest that the theoretical basis of ethnicity studies is still moving in the shadow of cultural primordial principles, without any real ability to break through to synthesize aspects that proved their presence and importance in the lives of the people, as shown in this account of the shantytown community of Al-Baraka. I argue that the established constructivist position on identity, and the attempt to soften the term to avoid the claims of the essentialism through insisting that identities are constructed, fluid, and multiple, leaves us without a justification for talking about identities at all. Moreover, it means that we are ill-equipped to examine the hard dynamics and essentialist claims of contemporary identity politics. Soft constructivism allows assumed identities to develop, although as they flourish, the term loses its analytical power."If identity is everywhere, it is nowhere" (Brubaker and Cooper 2000: 1).

We have a strong need to combine the ethnic aspects of social analysis with other aspects that truly make a significant difference in the way in which people pursue their own lives. If we take the example of the Al-Baraka community, it seems that ethnic groups and ethnic organizations are not the only determinant factors in how people organize their lives. Issues related to their settlement in an urban environment affect their lives in ways that sometimes exceed the effects of ethno-cultural factors. The kinds of job available to individuals, assets, education, technology and gender all have a tremendous influence upon the lives of people, although we cannot include them satisfactorily if we use the concept of ethnic identity or identity politics due to their apparent limitations.

What we need is a more flexible concept that will include a wider range of factors. Thus, it seems that using social identity as a main concept has offered this study many advantages, as Brubaker and Cooper put it succinctly:

> "'Identity' too, is both a category of practice and a category of analysis. As a category of practice, it used by 'lay' actors in some (not all!) everyday settings to make sense of themselves, of their activities, of what they share with, and how they differ from, others. It is also used by political entrepreneurs to persuade people to understand themselves, their interests, and their predicaments in a certain way, to persuade certain people that they are (for certain purposes) "identical" with one another and at the same time different from others, and to organize and justify collective actions along certain lines. In these ways the term 'identity' is implicated both in everyday life and in 'identity politics' in its various forms" (Brubaker and Cooper 2000: 5).

Since using the concept of social identity would open the door for many expected or unexpected factors to be accounted for, there are no pre-assumed factors. However, we need to be aware that having a wider range of possibilities also requires some adjustment, to ensure it will not lead to vague results. In other words, if we use the concept of social identity in the same way that we used the concept of identity—where the range and focus of study is not clear—we might end up having unlimited numbers of factors, or indeed many different factors without being able to understand their complex relations. Consequently, there is a need to use different methodological tools to measure the application of this concept.

To overcome this problem, I believe that the method of focusing on the life practices and actions of people should be prominent, including the examination of the meanings, competences and materiality of social practices of daily life. In this sense, the focus might be shifted from only what people say or imagine about themselves, to what they do in their practiced life, whereby we could interpret their verbal definition according to their actions. This approach is consistent with the usage of social practices as the main criteria to categorize the lifestyle groups of the Al-Baraka community. According to this specific conceptualization of social identity, I tried to explore what kinds of activities and practices people pursue, subsequently weighing their own justifications of their actions and the meanings generated as part of their actions, rather than a determinant.

Another aspect in replacing ethnic identification with social identification is reducing the stress upon the essential aspects of social life, and opening the door for other factors to be accounted, without assuming them as irrelevant. I have tried to place the essential factors (e.g. ethnic origins, languages, religion) in their appropriate place, as well as understanding their relationships with other constructed factors (e.g. modernity, urbanization, gender), and looking more systematically at who exactly uses these factors and when.

Using the concept of social identity in analyzing the Al-Baraka community began in this thesis through examining the social structure of the community. Consequently, I tried to develop the concept of lifestyle as a bundle of specific sets of practices and values adopted by different social groups. The relationship between the lifestyle concept and the social identity concept lay in the ability of the former to reveal the practices of every sub-group and the different modes of meanings generated by different lifestyle groups. More precisely, social identity appears as an umbrella that includes all segments and lifestyle groups of a shantytown's population, while lifestyle deals with the everyday practices of those specific social groups. More importantly, the cross-cutting relations between the different lifestyles, and the ways in which people choose their specific mode of practice, seems vital to understanding the overall social identity of the community. As the example of Al-Baraka area has clearly shown, it is not possible to understand the shantytown's identity without understanding the practiced lifestyles of the three social lifestyles, and moreover without understanding the ways in which people choose their position on the lifestyle triangle.

8.5 How Identity and Lifestyles are Constructed

Returning to the initial questions, I will try to discuss here how identity and lifestyles are being constructed and re-constructed in Sudan, as informed by the example of Al-Baraka community.

In academic literature, Sudan is usually depicted as a country suffering from a 'crisis of identity', whereby this troubled identity is usually explained in the form of binary opposition on different bases, primarily ethnic: African vs. Arab, or religious: Islam vs. Christianity and traditional beliefs, as well as on a linguistic basis as Arabic vs. traditional languages.

This depiction has a certain amount of credibility, since it explains how the people of the north of Sudan use their culture as a hegemonic power to dominate the whole country, which has historically happened since Islam entered Sudan in the sixteenth century, as a religion and culture in the beginning, and followed by ethnic groups claiming Arab origin later on. Furthermore, even after the country gained its independence from British colonization, the same hegemonic group and culture continued its domination.

From the example of the identity and lifestyles drawn from Al-Baraka, using this binary opposition theory to explain the relations between shantytown settlers and the rest of the city might also explain part of local relations. Nonetheless, what is missing here is the role of the city as a realm of modernity, including the role of the modern state in facilitating and maintaining the dominance of certain ideology claimed by certain people, in a sense that without the overarching power of the modern state and its ubiquitous institutions and values, it might not be possible for this specific ethnic groups to continue its domination.

For this purpose, it becomes inevitable that beside the cultural stuffs (using Fredrick Barth's apt concept, Barth 1970) or the primordial basis of identification following Eriksson's typology (Eriksson 1993), there are wide ranges of values, practices, institutions belonging to and initiated through modernity and the invention of the modern state and urbanity that should be considered as a fundamental part of the identity of the local people. However, we need to be very aware of the fact that what we are talking about here is localized modernity, or a domesticated modern state, and certainly a locally modified urbanity, which are very different from the old types introduced through colonization and other normal diffusion methods.

Importantly, lifestyles are the carriers of new values and institutions that stem from modernity and urbanization. These lifestyles express themselves through social practices, which involve diverse meanings, materiality and competences. Each lifestyle is constituted of a bundle of specific social practices that invoke certain meanings through different material objects, comprising specific criteria of competences.

All this means that urbanization, or being part of the city for shantytown dwellers, is not a mere act of inclusion or exclusion, but rather part of a social identity expressed through certain lifestyle practices. For shantytown settlers, the practices of being an African, speaking a home area language, or having a belief in one's ancestor religion are not only the determinant of someone's identity, but also being and becoming a shantytown settler as their complete social identity.

8.6 The Localization of Social Identity

As mentioned in the last chapter, it is possible to use the concept of localization—instead of assimilation—to interpret the whole process of adoption and internalization of different kinds of institutions and sets of practices by local people from different sources. This happened within the realms of lifestyles, where every lifestyle group tried to adopt ideas and practices as much as possible to establish their legitimacy and attract more people to join them in their specific lifestyle and social world.

It is possible to develop this idea and use it to interpret a wider situation, namely the congregation of lifestyles adopted by people, or their whole social identity. Indeed, when we try to make a generalization about the whole population of the shantytowns, in fact, we are talking about localization on a community scale, or more precisely about the shantytowns vis-à-vis other communities.

Practically, this means initially at least when local people interact with themselves and the environment around them, they encounter other identities (i.e. different lifestyles) from their original areas, urban surroundings or even from the outside world through technology and media. However, none of these proposed identities could satisfy their exact needs, but remain sources of a specific identity under construction and localization.

People used their agency to move freely between those different options, or more precisely different groups, making their choices according to their needs by modifying and localizing the different sets of identities through their social practices. Ultimately, they craft a new invented identity (through practiced lifestyles) based upon all the different options available and already adopted by various lifestyle groups.

The invention of a shantytown social identity, according to this analysis, is a result of continuous interactions and exchanges between the local community and outside world(s). Through different local social groups and specific lifestyles engaged in endless localization processes, the ultimate result is a sort of social identity unique to all world(s) that contributed to the existence of the shantytown. The localization of the identity of the shantytown community is the nucleus example of what is happening in all different communities in Sudan or the global South in general.

Accordingly, the social identity of Sudan today is certainly not confined to the simplistic binary opposition (e.g. Arab vs. African); rather, it is constituted of a social identity comprised from more complex sets of practiced lifestyles. Those practiced lifestyles are informed and communicated with all the world(s) that they have been related to in the past or in the present.

References

Abdalla, Muna Ahmed (2008): *Poverty and Inequality in Urban Sudan: Policies, Institutions and Governance*. Leiden: African Studies Center.

Abdul-Jalil, Musa Adam (1985): The Dynamics of Ethnic Identification in Northern Darfur. In: Beshir, Mohamed Omer (ed.): *The Sudan: Ethnicity, Regionalism and National Cohesion*. Bayreuth African Studies Series 1.

Abdul-Jalil, Musa Adam, Adam Azzain and A. A. Yousuf (2007): Future Prospects for Native Administration and Local Governance in Darfur. In A. De Waal (ed.): *War in Darfur and the Search for Peace, Global Equity Initiative*. Harvard University.

Abusharaf, Rogaia Mustafa (2009): *Transforming Displaced Women in Sudan: Politics and the body in a squatter settlement.* Chicago: The University of Chicago Press.

Ahmad, Adil Mustafa (1989): Housing Submarkets for the Urban Poor—the Case of Greater Khartoum, the Sudan. *Environment and Urbanization* 1 (2): 50-59.

Akoy, Akoy Dual (1994): *The Education of the Southern Sudanese Displaced in Khartoum.* Unpublished Master Thesis. Khartoum: University of Khartoum.

Assal, M. (2009): The Question of dentity in the Sudan: New dimensions for an old problem". *The Maghreb Review* 34 (2–3): 181-194.

Assal, Munzoul A. M. (2006): *Whose Rights Count? National and international responses to the rights of IDPs in the Sudan.* Brighton: Development Research Center on Migration, Globalisation and Poverty, University of Sussex.

Assal, Munzoul (2006): Sudan: Identity and Conflict over Natural Resources. *Development* 49 (3).

Assal, Munzoul (2008): *Urbanization and the Future of Sudan*. Khartoum: Unpublished paper.

Bakhit, Abdel Hamid (1994): Availability, Affordability and Accessibility of Food in Khartoum. *GeoJournal* 34 (3): 253-255.

Bakhit, Mohamed (2013): From Illegal Squatter Settlement towards Legal Shantytowns: Negotiations of power and responsibilities in Khartoum shantytowns". In: *BIGSASworks! 11*: 7-21. Also available online on: https://epub.unibayreuth.de/113/1/BIGSASworks_4_05oct2013.pdf

Banks, Marcus (1996): *Ethnicity: Anthropological constructions.* London: Routledge.

Bannaga, Mahmoud Yousif (1987): Family and Community Life in a Housing Estate: El-Sha'abiya, Khartoum North. In: Mohamed A Mohamed-Salih and Margaret A Mohamed-Salih (eds.): *Family Life in Sudan.* Khartoum: Graduate College Publications, University of Khartoum.

Bannaga, Sharaf Eldin Ibrahim (2001): *The Displacements and the Chances of Peace.* Khartoum: African University Press.

Bannaga, Sharaf Eldin Ibrahim (2000): *Al-Shorouk: The Organization of villages in the state of Khartoum.* Zurich: The Ministery of Engineering Affairs State of Khartoum in collaboration with the Habitat Group at the Swiss Federal Institute of Technology.

Barth, Fredrik (1970) (ed.): *Ethnic Group and Boundaries: The social organization of Culture difference.* London: George Allen and Unmin.

Baumann, Gerd (1980): Social and Cultural Constellations in Rural Development: A case study from the Nuba Mountains (South Kordofan). In: Post-Independence Sudan-Proceeding of a Seminar held in the Center of African Studies, University of Edinburgh, 21st and 22nd November 1980-Center of African Studies, University of Edinburgh, 1981.

Beck, Kurt (1998): Tribesmen, Townsmen and the Struggle over Proper Lifestyle in Northern Kordofan. In: Endre Stiansen and Michael Kevane (eds.): *Kordofan Invaded: Peripheral incorporation and social transformation in Islamic Africa*. Leiden: Brill, 254-279.

Beck, Kurt (2009): The Art of Truck Modding on the Nile (Sudan): An attempt to trace creativity. In: Jan-Brat Gewald, Sabine Luning and Klaas van Walraven (eds.): *The Speed of Change: Motor vehicles and people in Africa, 1890-2000.* Leiden: Brill.

Brubaker, Rogers and Frederick Cooper (2000): Beyond 'Identity'. *Theory and Society* 29:1-47.

Bruce, Steve and Steven Yearley (2006): *The Sage Dictionary of Sociology*. London: SAGE Publications Ltd.

CARE and International Office for Migration (2003): Sudan IDP Demographic, Socio-Economic Profiles for Return and Reintegration Planning Activities: Khartoum IDP Households, 2003. Survey conducted by Care and IOM.
Available at:
<http://www.internaldisplacement.org/8025708F004CE90B/%28httpDocments%29/4DCEA6D0F8B73CAF802570B7005A56C7/$file/CARE+IOM+Khartoum+Survey+FEb03.pdf>.

Central Bureau of Statistics (2009): *Statistical Yearbook for the Year 2009.* Khartoum: Central Bureau of Statistics.

Christiansen, Catrine, Mats Utas and Henrik E. Vigh (1996) (eds.): *Navigating Youth, Generating Adulthood: Social becoming in an African context.* Uppsala: Nordiska Afrikainstitutet.

Cohen, Abner (1981): *The Politics of Elite Culture: Explorations in the dramaturgy of power in a modern African society.* Los Angeles: University of California Press.

Creswell, John W. (1998): *Qualitative Inquiry and Research Design: Choosing among five traditions.* New York: Sage Publication, Inc.

Davies, H.R.J. and R.P.D. Walsh (1997): Historical Changes in the Flood Hazard at Khartoum, Sudan: Lessons and warnings for the future. *Singapore Journal of Tropical Geography* 18 (2): 123-40.

Davis, Mike (2006): *Planet of Slums.* London: Verso Press.

De Boeck, Philip and Alcinda Honwana (2005): Children and Youth in Africa: Agency, identity and place." In: Philip De Boeck and Alcinda Honwana (eds.): *Makers and Breakers: Children and youth in post-colonial Africa.* Dakar: Africa World Press.

De Geoffroy, Agnes (2009): Fleeing War and Relocating to the Urban Fringe—Issues and Actors: The cases of Khartoum and Bogota. *International Review of the Red Cross.* 91 (875): 509-526.

De Waal, A. (2005): Who are the Darfurians? Arab and African identities, violence and external engagement. *African Affairs* 104 (415): 181-205.

Deng, Francis M. (1995): *War of Visions: Conflict of identities in the Sudan.* Washington, DC: Brookings Institution.

Deng, Francis M. (2005): African Renaissance: Towards a New Sudan. *Forced Migration Review* 24.

El Dawi, Tajel Anbia Ali (1972): Sudan Urban Society. In: *Urbanization* (Conference paper). Khartoum: Philosophical Association.

El-Hassan, Idris Salim (2007): Urban *Violence in Greater Khartoum and Prospects of Peace in the Sudan.* Unpublished paper: Khartoum.

Elias, Badri Omer and Hassan Yassin Bedawi (1972): The Squatter Housing Problem: A review of government policy and solutions." In: *Urbanization* (Conference paper). Khartoum: Philosophical Association.

El-Kheir, Osman Mohamed (1991): Unauthorized Settlements in Greater Khartoum. In: M.E. Abu Sin and H.R.J. Davies (eds.): *The Future of Sudan's Capital Region: A study in development and change.* Khartoum: Khartoum University Press.

Eltigani, Eltigani E. (1995) (ed.): *War and Drought in Sudan: Essays on population displacement.* Florida: University Press of Florida.

Epstein, A.L. (1967): Urbanization and Social Change in Africa. *Current Anthropology* 8 (4).

Epstein, A.L. (1992): *Scenes from African Urban Life: Collected Copperbelt Papers.* Edinburgh: Edinburgh University Press.

Eriksen, Thomas Hylland (1993):The Epistemological Status of the Concept of Ethnicity. In: *The Anthropology of Ethnicity* (Conference paper). Amsterdam.

Eriksen, Thomas Hylland (1993): *Ethnicity and Nationalism: Anthropological perspectives.* London: Pluto Press.

Galal-al-Din, Mohamed El-Awad (1980): The Nature and Causes of Labour Migration to the Khartoum Conurbation. In:,Valdo Pons (ed.): *Urbanization and Urban Life in the Sudan.* Khartoum: DSRC—Development Studies and Research Center, 434-444.

Geschiere, Peter, Birgit Meyer and Peter Pels (2008) (eds.): *Reading in Modernity in Africa.* London: The International African Institute School of Oriental and African Studies.

Gore, Paul Wani (1998): The Socio-Economic and Demographic Consequences of Population Displacement in Sudan. In: Medani Mohamed M. Ahmed: *Current Studies on the Sudan.* Omdurman: Mohamed Omer Bashir's Center for Sudanese Studies.

Hale, Sondra Dungan (1979): *The Changing Ethnic Identity of Nubians in an Urban Milieu: Khartoum, Sudan.* A dissertation for the degree Doctor of Philosophy in Anthropology. Los Angeles: University of California.

Hannerz, Ulf (1980): *Exploring the City: Inquiries towards an urban anthropology.* New York: Columbia University Press.

Hebdige, Dick (2002): *Subculture: The meaning of style.* London and New York: Routledge.

Ibrahim, Fouad N. (1990): The Conditions of the Southern Sudanese Women Migrants in Abu Siid Shanty Town, Omdurman, Sudan—A case study of cultural change. *GeoJournal* 20 (3): 249-258.

Idris, Amir H. (2005): *Conflict and Politics of Identity in Sudan.* Palgrave Macmillan.

James, Wendy (1980): The Shanty Towns of Port Sudan. In: Valdo Pons (ed.): *Urbanization and Urban Life in the Sudan.* Khartoum: DSRC—Development Studies and Research Center.

Kenyon, Susan M. (2004): *Five Women of Sennar*. Illinois: Waveland Press, Inc.

Lewis, Oscar (1988): The Culture of Poverty. In: George Gmelch and Walter P. Zenner (eds.): *Urban Life: Readings in Urban Anthropology.* USA: Waveland Press.

Lloyd, Peter C. (1979): Shantytowns in Developing Nations. *Current Anthropology* 20 (1).

Loyal, Steven and Barry Barnes (2001): "Agency" as a Red Herring in Social Theory. *Philosophy of the Social Sciences* 31: 507-524.

Mac Gee, R. Jon and Richard L. Warms (1996): *Anthropological Theory: An introductory history.* California: Mayfield Publishing Company.

Makris, G. P. (1996): Slavery, Possession and History: The construction of the self among slave descendants in the Sudan. *Africa:* 66 (2): 159-182.

Manger Leif, O. (1994): *From the Mountains to the Plain: The integration of the Lafofa Nuba into Sudanese society.* Uppsala: the Scandininavian Institute of African Studies.

Manger, Leif O. (1987) (ed.): *Communal Labour in the Sudan.* Bergen: University of Bergen.

Mayer, Philip (1971): *Townsmen or Tribesmen: Conservatism and the process of urbanization in a South African City.* Cape Town: Oxford University Press.

Mazrui, Ali. A. (1971): The Multiple Marginality of the Sudan. In: Yusuf Fadl Hassan (ed.): *Sudan in Africa.* Khartoum: University of Khartoum Press.

Merghani, Rehab Elzeber Abd-Elatif (1998): *Al Haj Yousif Town: Comparative empirical study of types of settlements during 1996-1998.* Unpublished Master Thesis (in Arabic). Khartoum: University of Khartoum.

Mukhtar, Al-Baqir al-Afif (2005): The Crisis of Identity in Northern Sudan: A dilemma of a black people with a white culture. In: C. Fluehr-Lobban and K. Rhodes (eds.): *Race and Identity in the Nile Valley: Ancient and Modern Perspectives.* Trenton, NJ: The Red Sea Press.

Neubert, Dieter (2014): What is 'Middle Class'? In search for an appropriate concept. *Middle East—Topics & Arguments (META)* 2: 23-35.

Nilsson, Desiree (2000): *Internally Displaced, Refugees and returnees from and in the Sudan: A review.* Uppsala: Nordiska Afrikainstitutet.

Njoh, Ambe J. (2009): Ideology and Public Health Elements of Human Settlement Policies in Sub-Saharan Africa. *Cities* 26: 9-18.

O'Fahey, R.S. (2008): *The Darfur Sultanate: A history.* London: HURST Publishers Ltd.

O'Fahey, R.S. (1996): Islam and Ethnicity in Sudan. *Journal of Religion in Africa* 26 (3).

Pantuliano, Sara, Munzoul Assal et al. (2011): *City Limits: Urbanization and vulnerability in Sudan, Khartoum Case Study.* London: Overseas Development Institute.

Pekkinen, Jennifer (2009): Sudanese Elites: How the Riverain groups achieved political Dominance and their impact on the Sudanese state. *African Studies Program Paper*: 1-33.
Available at:
http://www.learningace.com/doc/1035921/8efc6f21223aed76d0c8532fde5e8118/jennifer-pekkinen-program-paper.

United Nations, Department of Economic and Social Affairs: Population Division, Population Estimates and Projections Section. 2012: *World Population Prospects: The 2012 Revision.*
Online database: http://esa.un.org/unpd/wup/unup/p2k0data.asp.

Republic of Sudan, Central Bureau of Statistics (2008): *National Census 2008.* Available via http://www.cbs.gov.sd.

Salih, M.A. Mohamed (1987): The Crescent, the Cross and the Devil's Flute: Islam and the present political turmoil in the Sudan. A Lecture Presented at the University of Lund, 1 October 1987.

Salih, M.A. Mohamed (1989): Anthropological and Sociological Research on Development and Social Change in the Sudan. In: Seyoum G. Selassie and El-Wathig Kameir (eds.): *Teaching and Research in Anthropology and Sociology in Eastern Africa Universities.* Addis Ababa: OSSREA Book Series.

Sanders, Jimy M. (2002): Ethnic Boundaries and Identity in Plural Societies. *Annu. Rev. Sociology* 28: 327-57.

Schlyter, Ann and Thomas Schlyter (1980): *George: The development of a squatter settlement in Lusaka, Zambia.* Stockholm: Swedish Council for Building Research.

Sharkey, Heather J. (2007): Arab Identity and Ideology in Sudan: The politics of language, ethnicity, and race. *African Affairs.* 107 (426).

Shove, Elizabeth, Mika Pantzar and Matt Watson (2012): *The Dynamics of Social Practice: Everyday life and how It changes.* London: Sage Publication Ltd.

Sikainga, Ahmed Alawad (1996): *Slaves into Workers: Emancipation and labor in colonial Sudan.* Austin: University of Texas Press.

Strauss, Anselm and Corbin, Juliet (1990): *Basics of Qualitative Research: Grounded theory procedures and techniques.* New York: Sage Publications.

Turner, Bryan S. (2006) (ed.): *The Cambridge Dictionary of Sociology.* Cambridge: Cambridge University Press.

United Nations Human Settlements Program (2003): *The Challenge of Slums: Global report on human settlement.* London: Earthscan Publications.

United Nations Human Settlements Programme (UN-Habitat) (2009): *Planning Sustainable Cities: Global report on human settlement 2009.* London: Earthscan.

Whyte, William Foote (1981): *Street Corner Society: The social structure of an Italian slum.* Chicago: The University of Chicago Press.

Yath, Yath Awan (1994*): The Dinka Immigrant in Gerief West, Khartoum, Sudan: Study on the local participation in the third world city.* PhD Thesis: University of Bayreuth.

Zahir, Fahima (1972): Khartoum North Squatter Settlements Urbanization, Migrant and Adjustment to the Urban Setting. In: *Urbanization*: Conference Paper. Khartoum: Philosophical Association.

Appendices

Appendix 1: Map for Quarter No. 2; Source: Local Committee, Quarter No. 2.

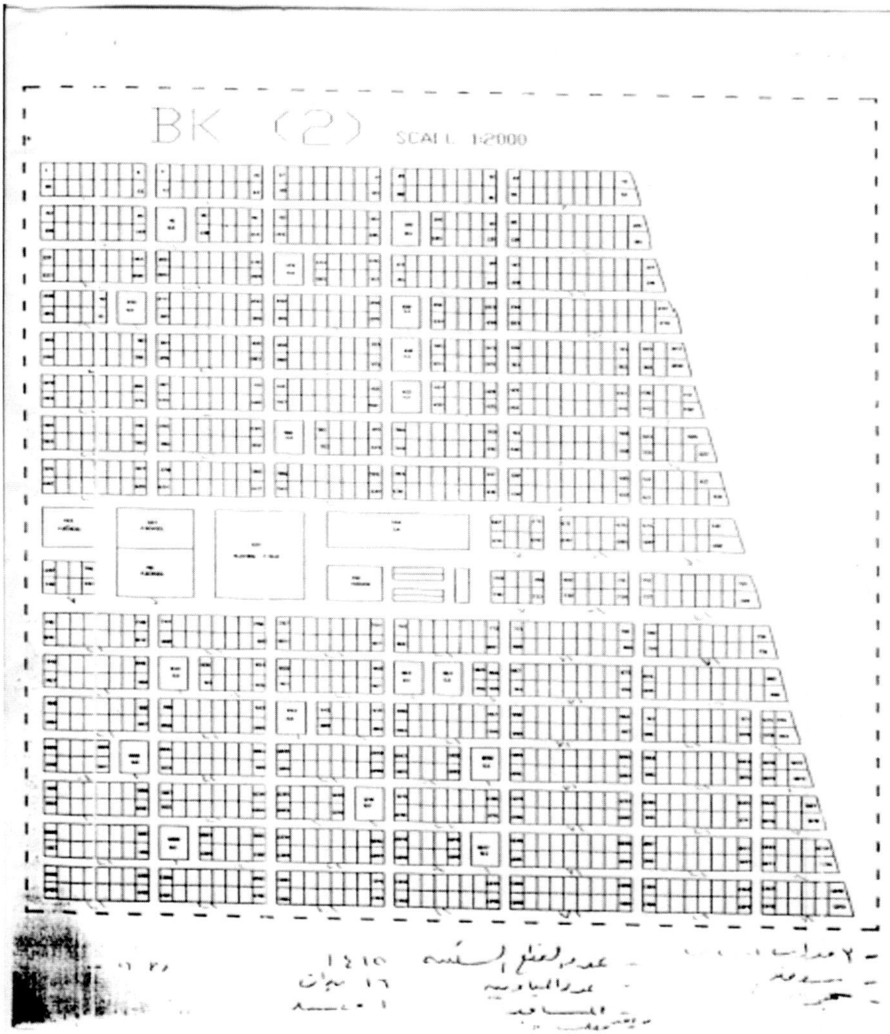

Description: Formal map illustrating the gridiron planning of Al-Baraka; the service area is located in the heart of the Quarter.

Appendix 2: Map of service area of Quarter No. 2; Source: Local Committee of Quarter No. 2.

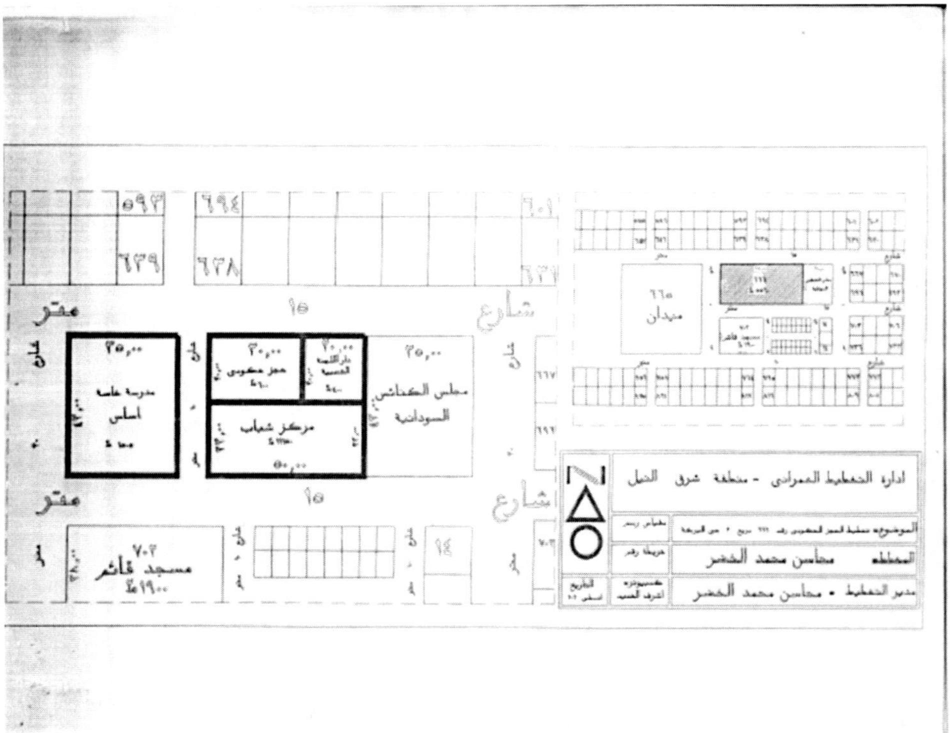

Description: Formal map produced by the Administration of Urban Planning - East Nile Locality. Illustrates the service area in Quarter No. 2 in detail, which includes, from left: primary private school, youth center, Local Committee house, and the Council of Sudanese Churches.

Appendix 3: Map of East Nile Unit;Source: Central Bureau of Statistics, Republic of Sudan.

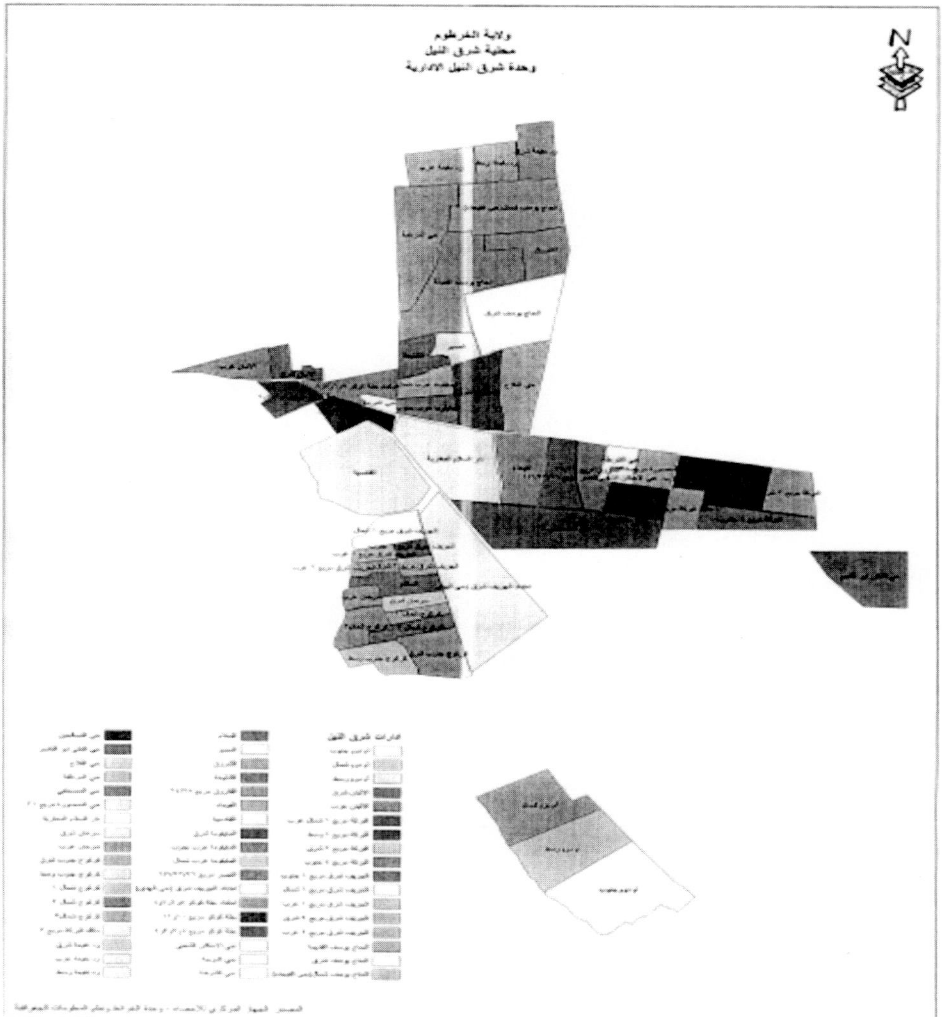

Description: Formal map of the East Nile Administrative Unit, which is part of East Nile Locality. Al-Baraka area belongs to this Administrative Unit. Remarkably, Al-Baraka is the only shantytown belonging to this Administrative Unit (in the far East); all other areas are rural villages and some lower middle class areas.

Appendix 4: Map of Haj Yousif Unit; Source: Central Bureau of Statistics, Republic of Sudan.

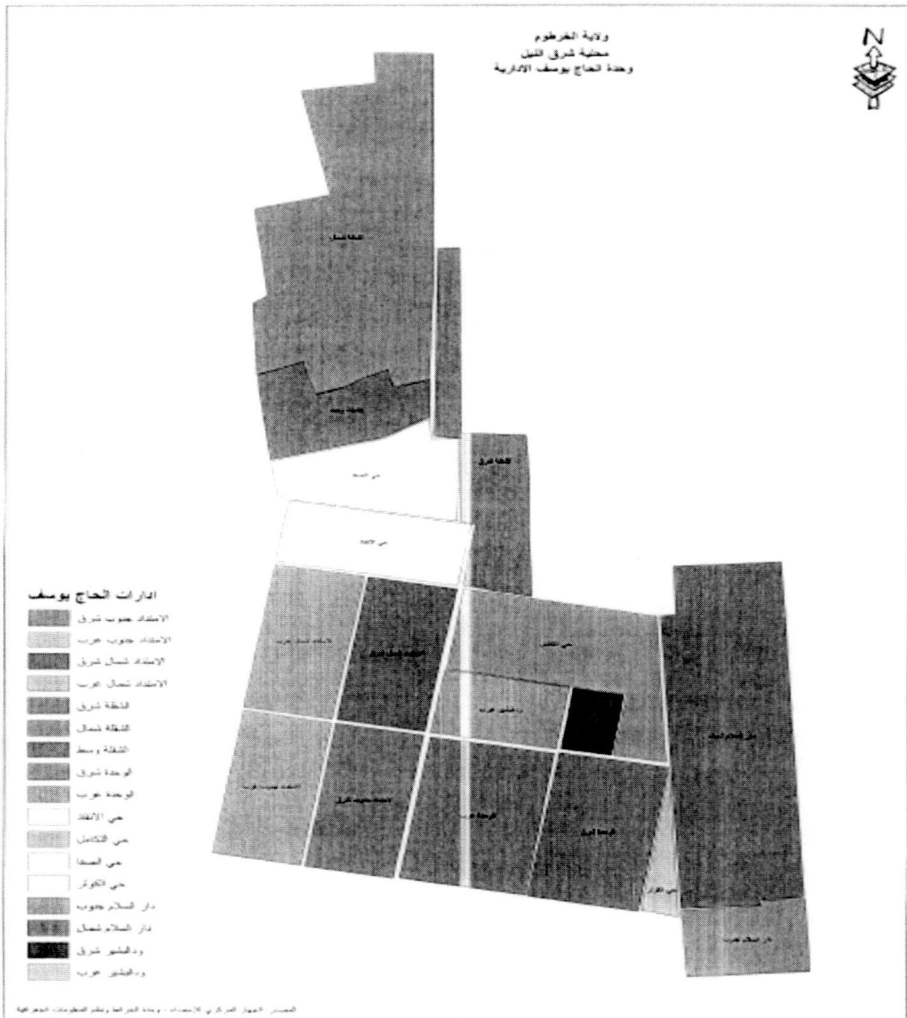

Description: Formal map of Haj Yousif Administrative Unit, which is the other part of East Nile Locality. The Wehda el Wataniya area belongs to this Administrative Unit. Notably, Al-Baraka is developed and planned as a part of Wehda el Wataniya shantytowns (in the far East). This division of shantytowns between the two Administrative Units was designed to weaken the power of the shantytowns in local government.

Appendix 5: Administrative Units of Khartoum State; Source: Central Bureau of Statistics, Republic of Sudan.

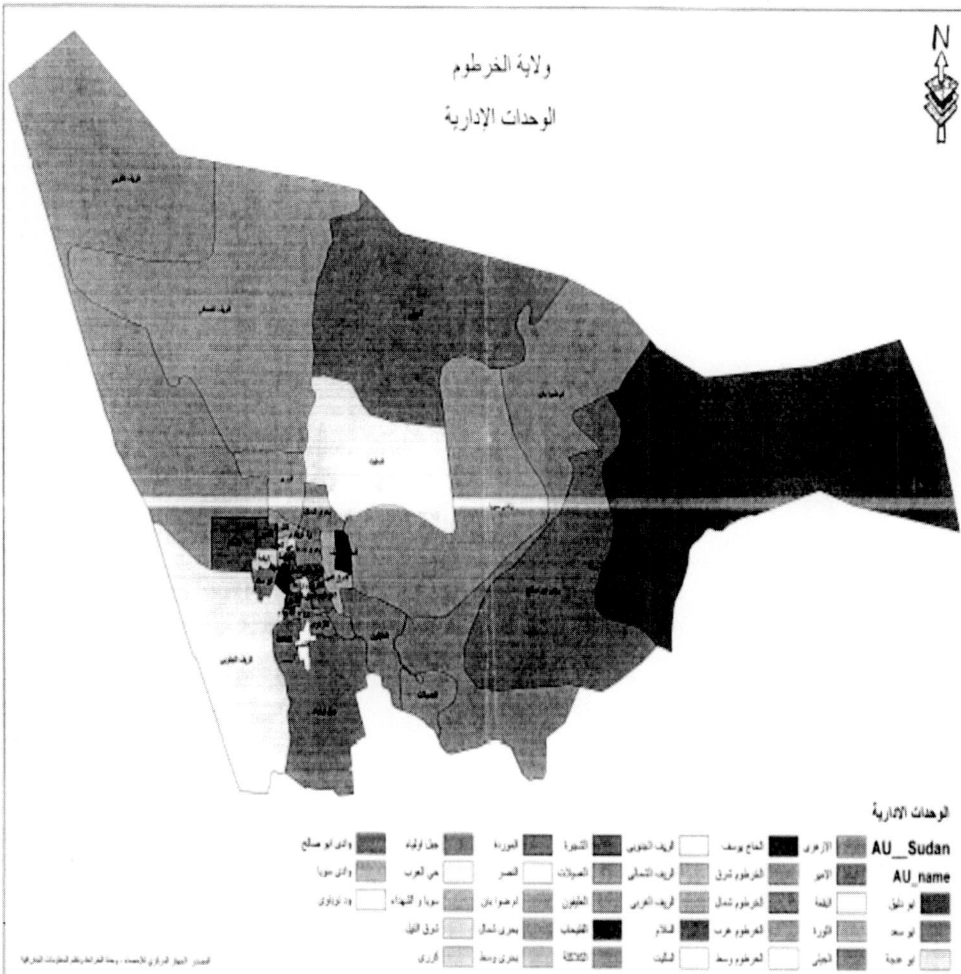

Description: This map illustrates all administrative units in Khartoum; it is clear that Wehda el Wataniya shantytowns are intentionally divided between the East Nile Administrative Unit and the Haj Yousif Administrative Unit.

Appendix 6: Sample of a rental contract; Source: First fieldwork period in Al-Baraka Quarter No.2.

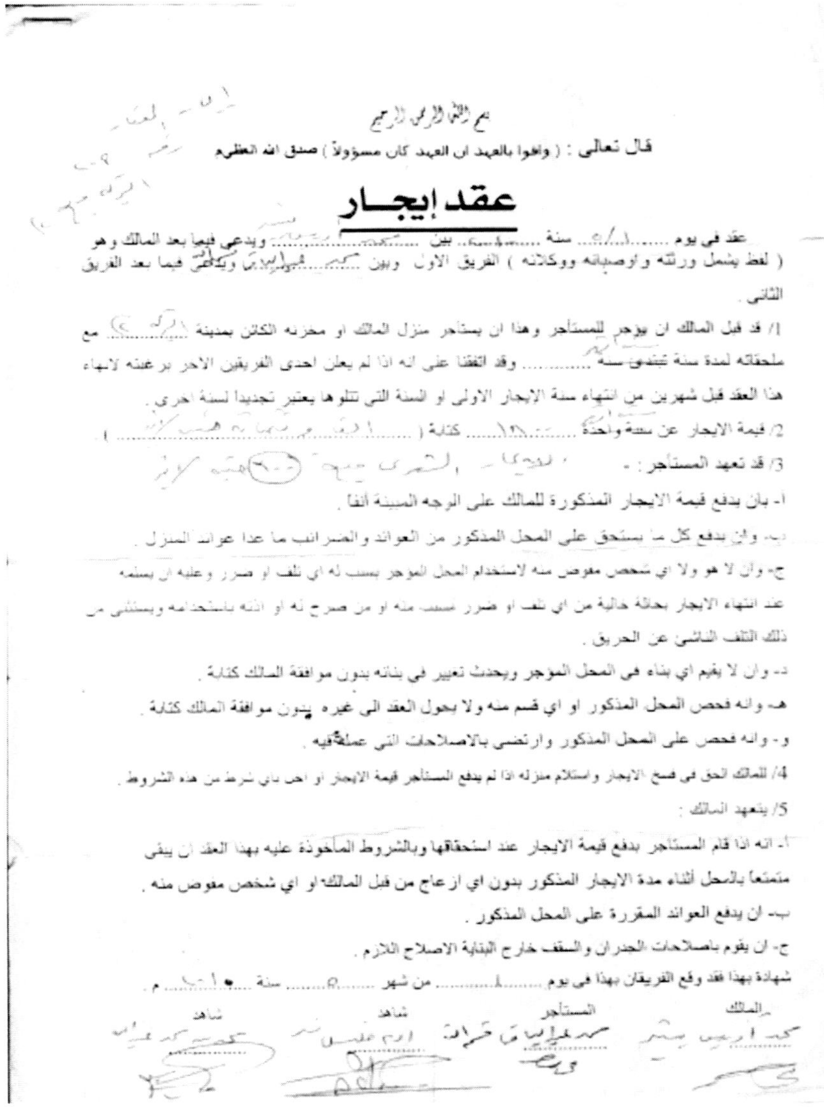

بسم الله الرحمن الرحيم

قال تعالى : (وأوفوا بالعهد ان العهد كان مسؤولاً) صدق الله العظيم

عقد إيجــار

عقد في يوم .... سنة .... بين .... ويدعى فيما بعد المالك وهو (لفظ يشمل ورثته واوصيائه ووكلائه) الفريق الاول وبين .... ويدعى فيما بعد الفريق الثاني .

1/ قد قبل المالك ان يؤجر للمستأجر وهذا ان يستأجر منزل المالك او مخزنه الكائن بمدينة .... مع ملحقاته لمدة سنة تبتدئ سنة .... وقد اتفقا على انه اذا لم يعلن احدى الفريقين الاخر برغبته لانهاء هذا العقد قبل شهرين من انتهاء سنة الايجار الاولى او السنة التي تتلوها يعتبر تجديدا لسنة اخرى .

2/ قيمة الايجار عن سنة واحدة .... كتابة (........) .

3/ قد تعهد المستأجر : -

أ- بان يدفع قيمة الايجار المذكورة للمالك على الوجه المبينة آنفا .

ب- وان يدفع كل ما يستحق على المحل المذكور من العوائد والضرائب ما عدا عوائد المنزل .

ج- وان لا هو ولا اي شخص مفوض منه لاستخدام المحل الموجر يسبب له اي تلف او ضرر وعليه ان يسلمه عند انتهاء الايجار بحالة خالية من اي تلف او ضرر تسبب منه او من صرح له او اذنه باستخدامه ويستثنى من ذلك التلف الناشئ عن الحريق .

د- وان لا يقيم اي بناء في المحل الموجر ويحدث تغيير في بنائه بدون موافقة المالك كتابة .

هـ- وانه فحص المحل المذكور او اي قسم منه ولا يحول العقد الى غيره بدون موافقة المالك كتابة .

و- وانه فحص على المحل المذكور وارتضى بالاصلاحات التي عملت فيه .

4/ للمالك الحق في فسخ الايجار واستلام منزله اذا لم يدفع المستأجر قيمة الايجار او اخل باي شرط من هذه الشروط .

5/ يتعهد المالك :

أ- انه اذا قام المستأجر بدفع قيمة الايجار عند استحقاقها وبالشروط المأخوذة عليه بهذا العقد ان يبقى متمتعا بالمحل أثناء مدة الايجار المذكور بدون اي ازعاج من قبل المالك او اي شخص مفوض منه .

ب- ان يدفع العوائد المقررة على المحل المذكور .

ج- ان يقوم باصلاحات الجدران والسقف خارج البناية الاصلاح اللازم .

شهادة بهذا فقد وقع الفريقان بهذا في يوم .... من شهر .... سنة .... م .

المالك	المستأجر	شاهد	شاهد

Description: This my rental contract for six months, describing all the legal binding obligations for the two parties. Note that the first witness for the contract is the secretary of the local committee of Quarter No. 2. Furthermore, the stamp on the contract belongs to the local committee of Quarter No. 2.